Navigating Social Security Disability in Illinois

By: Shawn M. Good &
Neil H. Good

Navigating Social Security Disability in Illinois
Copyright © 2018 Shawn M. Good & Neil H. Good

DISCLAIMER:
This book was written to provide readers with an overview of the
Social Security process and help them make informed decisions.
This book is not intended to be legal advice, nor is it intended to
establish an attorney-client relationship. If you or a loved one is
considering applying for Social Security benefits, we strongly
encourage you to contact our office for a free consultation: 847-
250-9183.

Better to remain silent and be thought a fool than to speak and to remove all doubt.

— ABRAHAM LINCOLN

Table of Contents

Chapter 1

What is Social Security Disability?

Social Security Disability Insurance ("SSDI") is a government-run disability insurance program administered by the Social Security Administration. Every paycheck you have ever received had Federal Insurance Contributions Act tax ("FICA") taken out to fund the SSDI program. Think of SSDI like car insurance. You only have car insurance if you paid the premium. Likewise, you are only eligible for SSDI benefits if you paid the tax.

To qualify, you must have paid into a sufficient number of quarters of coverage based on your age. Generally, the term 'quarters of coverage' refers to a three-month calendar quarter. If you are awarded benefits, you will receive monthly deposits. The amount of money you are eligible to receive is based on the amount of money you paid toward FICA. There are no asset limits to be eligible for SSDI. The minimum for SSDI is $735 per month, and the maximum is $2,687 per month as of 2017.

SSDI Quick Notes

Benefits for disabled individuals, widows, and some relatives

The amount of benefits you receive depends on the amount of F.I.C.A. tax you have paid

2017 - Maximum cash benefits: $2,687

2017 - Countable resources are **NOT** relevant for individuals seeking to obtain SSDI

The onset date is the date you stop working due to your disability limiting your ability to work full-time

Individuals are eligible for Medicare 29 months after their onset date

What is Supplemental Security Income (SSI)?

The other program the Social Security Administration (SSA) supervises is the Supplemental Security Income program (SSI). SSI is often confused with SSDI, but the two are very different. SSDI and SSI have quite similar names, but these government programs have significant differences.

Supplemental Security Income (SSI) and Social Security Disability Insurance (SSDI) are two distinctive programs and it is important for potential applicants to know the differences between the two. SSI is a needs-based program and is funded by the government and is financed by the general revenues of the U.S. Treasury Department. SSI benefits are not related to an applicant's work record like SSDI benefits. SSI pays eligible individuals or couples a fixed amount of money per month, though the specific amount may be lowered depending on whether an applicant has work income. SSI pays benefits to low-income people at the age of 65 or older, to disabled or blind adults, and disabled or blind children. However, because of its strict financial requirements, SSI is only available to persons with limited assets and income. To qualify, you must have less than $2,000, excluding your home and your car. SSI is for individuals who have not paid FICA tax, or who do not currently have enough quarters of coverage to qualify for SSDI. As of 2018, the maximum benefits you can receive, if you are awarded SSI, is $750 a month, along with Medicaid.

Eligibility for SSD and SSI Benefits

Determining eligibility for Social Security Disability Insurance (SSDI) or SSI benefits is largely based on your level of disability and your ability to hold gainful employment. If you are unable to work due to disability or illness and you meet the SSDI or SSI disability requirements, the assistance of an experienced lawyer may be vital in helping you obtain the benefits you need to provide a comfortable life for you and your family. More than 65% of SSDI applications are denied. When an application for SSDI is denied, you may file for reconsideration. At the reconsideration stage, which is the second step, 92% of applicants are denied.

According to a recent Congressional report, "Professional representation is a valuable, and indeed vital, service. The disability determination process is complex. Claimants without professional representation appear to be far less likely to receive the benefits to which they are entitled. For example, in 2000, 64% of claimants represented by an attorney, but only 40% of those without one, were awarded benefits at the hearing level."[1] If you are applying for benefits and are looking for an attorney to represent you or a loved one, please call our office at: (847)250-9183.

---

[1] November 16, 2001 Congressional Record, Testimony of Member of Congress, Robert T. Matsui of California, discussing the Attorney Fee Payment System Improvement Act (2001).

TIP: If you or a loved one is thinking of applying for benefits, ALWAYS apply for both SSDI & SSI.

SSI – Quick Notes
These are benefits for elderly or disabled individuals who have little to no income
In 2017 the maximum cash benefits were$735 per month for individuals and $1,103 for couple
In 2017 the countable resources must **NOT** be worth more than $2,000 for an individual or $3,000 for a couple. Countable resources are the things you own that count toward the resource limit
You are also Eligible for Medicaid
The onset date is the date of application (there is no back-pay)
Living arrangements like free housing may affect benefit amounts/eligibility

You Cannot Receive Social Security Retirement and Disability Benefits Together

People who are eligible for both Social Security retirement benefits and disability benefits may wonder if they are allowed to collect these benefits at the same time. In general, you cannot receive Social Security Retirement and Disability benefits together, because the SSDI program is designed to provide benefits to people who are unable to work due to a disabling condition and who are not old enough to begin drawing their retirement benefits. As a result, Social Security Disability benefits are often thought of as retirement benefits for those who are forced to retire early because of a disability.

Social Security Disability benefits are converted to retirement benefits when you reach the age of retirement. While you cannot receive both Social Security Retirement and Disability benefits together, there is one important exception: the early retirement exception.

The Early Retirement Exception

The SSA allows people, starting at age 62, to take early reduced retirement benefits. In line with these early benefits, there is one exception to the rule above—one can take advantage of early retirement through the

Social Security system and could be approved for disability benefits later.

To qualify for this exception, you must have been disabled before your early retirement benefits started. If you drew less than a full retirement benefit for some amount of time and are later approved for disability benefits, the SSA will retroactively pay you the difference between the early retirement benefit and the full disability amount for the months you were disabled but only were receiving early retirement benefits.

Consider this example: A 62-year-old man must quit work because of health problems and begins collecting early retirement benefits. He later applies for disability benefits and is approved. The SSA believes his disability began before he started collecting early retirement benefits. As a result, the SSA will pay the man the difference between his disability payment and his early retirement payment for the months he only received early retirement benefits.

If the SSA determines that your disability started after you began receiving early retirement benefits or if the SSA denies your claim, they will not pay you any disability benefits, and you will continue to receive reduced early retirement payments for the rest of your life.

When to Take Early Retirement

Purposefully quitting work at age 62 to collect early retirement with the hope of also qualifying for disability benefits can be a gamble. It is very important to remember that there is no guarantee you will be awarded disability benefits. If you elect to take early retirement benefits and the SSA does not grant you disability benefits, you will be forced to collect less than your full retirement benefits for the rest of your life. While retiring early and applying for disability can work for those who are severely impaired before taking early retirement, it may not be the best plan for everyone.

Children & Supplemental Security Income (SSI)

Children may qualify for SSI disability benefits upon birth. There is no age requirement, and children may be eligible for benefits until they reach age 18. In Illinois, as well as many other states, children are eligible for Medicaid, which can help pay medical bills.[2] The 2017 income limit for benefits is $735 per month for an individual and $1,103 per month for a couple.

---

[2]https://www.illinois.gov/hfs/MedicalPrograms/AllKids/Pages/about.aspx

Are Your Dependents Eligible for SSDI Benefits?

If you receive SSDI benefits, certain members of your family may be eligible for dependent benefits. Eligible dependents can receive up to 50% of your monthly SSDI benefits, to a family maximum of 150% to 180%. If the total amount of benefits paid to all family members, including the SSDI recipient, exceeds the family maximum, each dependent's benefit amount will be reduced proportionately to remain within the cap. The disabled recipient's monthly benefit amount will not be reduced. It is important to note that dependent benefits are only paid to SSDI recipients. There are no dependent benefits associated with SSI.

Minor Children Dependent Benefits

If you have minor children, they will be eligible to receive dependent benefits if they are unmarried and meet one of the following criteria:

1. Are under the age of 18; or
2. Are age 18 or 19 and a full-time student

Dependent benefits end when the child turns 18 unless he is enrolled in an elementary or secondary school program (not college). If your child is enrolled in school, his dependent benefits will end when he graduates from school or two months after his 19th birthday—whichever occurs first.

Adult Children Dependent Benefits

Unmarried adult children (over the age of 18) of SSDI recipients are eligible for dependent benefits if they have a disability that occurred before turning age 22.

For example, if your child was born with cerebral palsy and meets the SSA's definition of disability, she will be entitled to receive dependent benefits. If, however, your child was involved in a car accident at age 31 that left her permanently disabled, she would not be eligible for dependent benefits.

Claiming SSDI Benefits Based on Your Ex-Spouse's Earnings Record

Spousal SSDI benefits are available to the spouses of people who qualify for SSDI benefits. However, spousal benefits may be available even after divorce. An individual may collect half the amount of the SSDI benefits his or her ex-spouse receives, provided certain criteria are met.

The SSA requires people to meet the following criteria to collect benefits based on the record of an ex-spouse:

- The marriage must have lasted at least 10 years
- The spouse seeking dependent's benefits must be at least 62 years old
- The spouse seeking the benefits cannot be remarried
- The spouse must not be eligible for a higher benefit amount based upon personal earning records or another person's earning record

These are the only criteria the SSA considers. The age, health, employability and financial status of the dependent spouse are not taken into account.

An ex-spouse can collect benefits even if the spouse who receives SSDI payments remarries. The benefits awarded to the ex-spouse have no impact on the benefits the disabled spouse's current wife or husband, children, or other dependents receive. Similarly, the ex-spouse's benefits do not affect the disabled spouse's benefit amount.

If an ex-spouse who collected SSDI benefits passes away, the surviving spouse may be entitled to a survivors' benefit. A spouse may qualify if he or she is older than 60, older than 50 and disabled, caring for a minor child of the deceased spouse, or caring for a disabled child of the deceased spouse.

A surviving ex-spouse may collect anywhere from 75 to 100 percent of the deceased spouse's benefit amount. An ex-spouse claiming benefits based on a living spouse's record may receive 50 percent of the benefit amount. However, if the spouse seeking benefits receives a pension from work that Social Security does not cover, such as government work, the benefit amount may be reduced.

How to Apply for SSDI & SSI

There are four ways to apply for Social Security benefits. You can apply in-person, online, by phone or by traditional paper mail. There are pros and cons to all four ways.

If you need to apply today you may go online and apply at any time. You can do this at your leisure. If you get stuck with something or if you are too sick to finish at one time, an online application allows you to go at your own pace. You can login and log out over multiple sessions or even days.

An in-person application can be beneficial because there is an SSA employee asking you the questions. So, if you get stuck the SSA representative can assist you.

If it is too difficult for you to go to a district office and you do not have a computer you can use, you can call and schedule a phone application. This is typically done in one sitting and this will give you a contact person at SSA. If you want to do a phone application, be aware that you may end up spending some time waiting on the phone to schedule an appointment and your appointment may be in a few weeks or even a month.

Last, but certainly not least, applicants can apply by paper mail. You can go to a district office and get a paper application or download one online and submit it via traditional mail.

How Social Security Disability Cases Work

This section addresses the stages and categories of the process. The better you understand them, the less you will be confused and the easier it will be to complete this process with confidence.

The process to obtain benefits boils down to five parts:

1.   Application/Filing for Benefits
2.   Reconsideration
3.   Administrative Law Judge Hearing
4.   Appeals Council
5.   Federal District Court

Most cases end at the third step, the Administrative Law Judge Hearing; however, our offices have seen an increase in the number of cases that are going to the Appeals Council and even to Federal Court.

What Documents You Must Complete After Applying: Adult Function Report, Work History Questionnaire, and a Medical Exam.

After you apply, three things will automatically happen. First, you will be sent an Adult Function Report and a Work History Questionnaire. The Adult Function Report will have SSA-3373-BK typed in the lower left-hand corner of the document. The purpose of the Adult Function Report is to give the SSA a one minute snapshot of what your daily life is like. You must complete this document and return it back to the SSA. Make sure you keep your answers short and only answer the question that is asked.

The Work History Questionnaire will have SSA-3369-BK typed in the lower left-hand corner of the document. The purpose of the Work History Questionnaire is to give the SSA the information it needs to classify your Past Relevant Work ("PRW"). Your PRW is used along with your age, education, physical and/or mental limitations to determine if you are disabled.

Once you apply, the SSA will request that you see one of its doctors. This doctor is called a Consultative Examiner. These exams typically range from 5 minutes to 1 hour. The examiner will send a report to the SSA that will help determine whether they should approve or deny your application for benefits.

TIP: Do not send any documents back to the SSA with a regular postage stamp. This increases the chances of it getting lost in the mail or at the SSA office. If you hire a law firm, have your attorney submit it to the SSA on your behalf. If you decide not to hire an attorney, you may want to require a signature upon the receipt of the package at the SSA. Our office sends documents electronically and via certified mail to the SSA to ensure documents arrive in a timely manner and do not get lost.

Chapter 2

Do You Qualify?

According to the SSA: "The law defines disability as the inability to engage in any substantial gainful activity (SGA) by reason of any medically determinable physical or mental impairment(s) which can be expected to result in death or which has lasted or can be expected to last for a continuous period of not less than 12 months."[3] Substantial Gainful Activity (SGA) refers to making a specific amount of money earned from working.

To qualify, you must have earned less than the monthly SGA amount the SSA has set. In 2018, the monthly SGA amount for statutorily (legally) blind individuals is $1970, and for non-blind individuals, the monthly SGA amount is $1180.

---

[3] https://www.ssa.gov/disability/professionals/bluebook/general-info.htm

Below is a list of the monthly SGA amounts from 2005 to 2018.[4]

Year	Blind	Non-blind
2005	$1,380	$830
2006	1,450	860
2007	1,500	900
2008	1,570	940
2009	1,640	980
2010	1,640	1,000
2011	1,640	1,000
2012	1,690	1,010
2013	1,740	1,040
2014	1,800	1,070
2015	1,820	1,090
2016	1,820	1,130
2017	1,950	1,170
2018	1,970	1,180

---

[4] https://www.ssa.gov/oact/cola/sga.html

Medical Requirements

In order to obtain benefits, you must have a "medically determinable physical or mental impairment" that can be proven by "medically acceptable clinical and laboratory diagnostic techniques."[5] In other words, you need to go to the doctor, and your doctor must have records of your visits. Furthermore, the records must show you have a medical condition that limits your ability to work. Documentation is extremely important as you cannot simply say you have a bad back and can't work. The SSA will need to see proof from your doctor that backs up your claim. It is helpful to have medical records from the onset date, or as soon thereafter as possible. Additionally, pre-onset records can be helpful in terms of chronic or latent conditions.

TIP: The more records you have documenting current and consistent medical treatment and shows you cannot work, the stronger your case will be.

Vocational Requirement

After considering the medical evidence, the SSA will look to see what functional work limitations you have due to your medical conditions. Some examples of what the SSA looks at include your ability to stand,

---

[5] https://www.ssa.gov/disability/professionals/bluebook/general-info.htm

walk, sit, lift, carry, push, pull, crouch, kneel, and crawl.

TIP: Tell your doctors specific numbers, including how long you can sit, stand, walk, and how much you can carry. Having these numbers in your medical records will strengthen your case. Without your doctor writing down the numbers, the SSA will have to infer numbers based on the records they have. Without this specific information available, the limitations inferred could be minimal and, therefore, not help you win your benefits.

How Age is Factored In

Disabled workers can qualify for Social Security Disability benefits after they turn 18, if they meet other eligibility criteria. While many people believe this is the only way age affects their claims, in actuality, the SSA uses age categories and age-based assumptions to evaluate whether a person qualifies for a medical-vocational allowance, as well. If a person does not qualify for disability benefits by meeting an impairment listing, the person's age may be decisive.

Age As A Limiting Factor

Age can significantly impact a disabled worker's ability to train for or adjust to a new type of work. The SSA presumes older age creates greater constraints. It recognizes the following age categories and presumed limitations:

- Younger person — People between the ages of 18 and 49 are typically considered capable of learning new types of work. However, the SSA recognizes that people between ages 45 and 49 may be more limited than other younger individuals.

- Person closely approaching retirement age — People between ages 50 and 54- may be found incapable of pursuing new work, provided they have significant impairments or limited educations.

- Person of advanced age — Age is considered a substantial limiting factor for people 55 and older. The SSA also establishes special rules for people over age 60, or people closely approaching retirement age. These individuals are only considered capable of light work if their transferable skills are directly applicable to the work in question.

Due to the use of these age categories, the timing of an individual's SSDI application and claim evaluation can significantly affect the final decision.

Borderline Age Situations

The SSA allows special consideration for borderline age situations. If an individual is within days or months of joining a different age category, the claims examiner may evaluate the claim under the older category. This is only permitted if evaluation under the older category would result in a different outcome.

The SSA notes that few situations justify the use of an older category for an individual who is a year from the relevant birthday. To support evaluation under an older age category, a claims examiner must consider whether the applicant faces vocational adversities that the medical vocational guidelines do not recognize.

Minor vocational adversities, one month from an age change, may justify use of a higher age category if the individual's age is close to that category. Significant adversities are necessary if the age difference is large, such as 11 months from an age change. The law has a lot of gray areas regarding age; therefore, it is in this area that judges are given quite a bit of interpretational discretion. Providing detailed documentation of vocational adversities is essential for SSDI applicants whose age falls into the latter two groups of the SSA age categories.

Chapter 3

Why You Need a Lawyer and Not an Advocate!

In this chapter, we will go over questions everyone should ask before hiring an attorney. Choosing the right individual to represent you in your Social Security Disability case is one of the most important decisions you will make. What you need to know is that not all attorneys/legal advocates are equal.

You worked your whole life and paid a lot of taxes to be eligible for Social Security Disability benefits. Not all companies that handle Social Security Disability cases have attorneys working for them. Do not be fooled by "Nationwide Advocate Groups." Despite having lesser credentials, non-attorney Advocates get paid the exact same amount as attorneys under the law.

These are the following requirements for becoming a non-attorney advocate:

1. Have a bachelor's degree from an accredited institution of higher education or at least four years of relevant professional experience, and either a high school diploma or General Education Development (GED) certificate.

2. Pass a written examination that the Social Security Administration (SSA) writes and administers, which tests the knowledge of the relevant provisions of the Social Security Act as well as the most recent developments in the SSA and court decisions affecting titles II for SSDI and XVI for SSI of the Act.

3. Secure and maintain continuous professional liability insurance or equivalent insurance, which the SSA determines to be adequate to protect claimants in the event of malpractice by the representative.

4. Undergo a criminal background check to ensure the representative's fitness to practice before us.

5. Demonstrate ongoing completion of continuing education qualified courses, including education regarding ethics and professional conduct, which are designed to enhance professional knowledge in matters related to entitlement to, or eligibility for, benefits based on disability under titles II and XVI of the Act.[6]

---

[6] https://ttps://secure.cpshr.us/ssa/About.asp

By contrast, to become an attorney, it usually takes 7 years of full-time study after high school.

The requirements for becoming an attorney are as follows:

1. Have a 4-year college degree from an accredited institution.

2. Complete a Juris Doctor (J.D.) degree from a law school accredited by the American Bar Association (ABA).

3. Pass a written bar exam administered by a state supreme court. The bar exam covers not only social security and administrative law, but also may cover evidence, tax, constitutional law, workers compensation, torts, contracts, and many more subjects.

4. Undergo a criminal background check to insure the attorney's fitness to practice law.

5. Demonstrate ongoing completion of continuing education in qualified courses, including education regarding ethics and professional conduct, which are designed to enhance professional knowledge in matters related to the practice of law.

Most attorneys also take courses in law school that cover evidence, trial advocacy, cross-examining witnesses and performing opening and closing arguments.

Also, it is important to note that when an Advocate commits malpractice and destroys your case, even if it's unintentional, there is not much you can do. In contrast, state bar associations heavily regulate attorneys, who can get in serious trouble if they commit malpractice.

Tough Questions Everyone Applying for SSDI/SSI Should Ask Their Potential Lawyer

Here are some of the most important questions you **should** ask an attorney before hiring her.

Ask: Is an attorney going to represent me in court?

Why: Understand that many workers' compensation firms have added Social Security Disability law to their practices. Firms that concentrate in workers' compensation or personal injury often have their employees take the non-attorney disability representative test and then represent you in court. You want an attorney, not a non-attorney advocate that works for a law firm to represent you.

Ask: Does the law firm handle Federal Court appeals?

Why: If you lose at your hearing, you have likely already waited 2 to 2.5 years to see a judge. The number of cases being lost at hearings and the appeals council is staggering. You **need** a law firm who can take your case the entire way through the process. When you sign a contract with an attorney who does not do federal court appeals, you need to ask yourself: What happens if you are denied at the hearing or the appeals council?

If you hire an attorney who does not have experience in federal court appeals, and you lose your case, an attorney who does federal court appeals is not likely to take on the rest of your case. She may be reluctant because federal court appeals are not easy, and are very time consuming. A new attorney may have to split the overall legal fees with the attorney who previously lost, which means the new attorney would get lower fees and still have to do a great deal of work to get your case appealed.

- **Side note**: Advocates cannot go to federal court, because they are not attorneys, so they often give up if they lose your case at hearing.

Ask: Does the firm have specialized Residual Functional Capacity (RFC) questionnaires or medical source statements for my conditions? (Please refer to page __ for a detailed explanation of medical source statements)

Why: This is very important because your medical records alone typically do not state your physical limitations, including how far you can walk, how much you can carry, how long you can sit, how long you can stand, and many more factors that determine whether or not you are disabled under Social Security's strict definition. An experienced disability attorney should have questionnaires for a wide variety of conditions.

Ask: Who is paying (advancing the cost) for the medical records?

Why: The evidence in a disability case consists primarily of the medical record. Courts need evidence to decide cases. When you hire a law firm that agrees to advance the cost for your medical records, the attorney believes you have a winnable case. No competent law firm would take on a failing case and advance the cost of the medical records, because if they lose, the client should not have to pay them back.

You want an attorney to advance the cost for your records and collect the records for you. Prices to obtain records can vary drastically from state-to-state. Sometimes, they can be hundreds of dollars. Collecting accurate, complete, and relevant records for court is important for your hearing.

Ask: Does the law firm submit a pre-hearing memorandum or other document to the judge summarizing the theory of my case?

Why: Administrative Law Judges (ALJs) who hear SSD cases handle thousands of cases a year. Each case has a minimum of a few hundred pages of medical evidence, with many cases having thousands. The pre-hearing memorandum is meant to help the judge save time. It should cite specific pieces of evidence in the record so the judge does not have to search for everything on his/her own. A pre-hearing memorandum makes the judge's job a bit easier, and you want a happy judge, not an overwhelmed judge!

Ask: When will I be assigned an attorney/advocate?

Why: Going with a nationwide disability advocate group is **risky**. This is because you do not know who is going to be with you at the hearing. The identity of your representative should not be a surprise right before your hearing starts. You are paying a lot of money, so you should know and trust the person representing you in court.

Ask: Does the prospective attorney/law firm practice other areas of law that may benefit from an SSD case?

Why: Practice areas like Workers Compensation, Personal Injury, and Medical Malpractice often settle cases for much larger sums of money than the fees awarded for winning an SSD case. The reason other practice areas can be a red flag is that firms sometimes use SSD clients to see if they have more profitable cases, such as Workers Compensation, Personal Injury, and Medical Malpractice. This often results in less attention being put toward the attorney's SSD cases. This is not always the case, so you should look at all aspects of an attorney's practice when evaluating whether he is a good fit for you and your case.

Ask: Who is filing the request for reconsideration and the request for hearing?

Why: When you hire an attorney, you are paying them 25% of your back pay (if you win) with a maximum total fee of $6,000. This is not a small sum of money, so when you hire a law firm, be sure you get your money's worth. While, it is true that your representative cannot file your initial application, she can, however, submit the request for reconsideration and request for a hearing on your behalf. It is nice to know that your attorney will handle this for you.

How Do You Pay Your Lawyer?

When you hire a disability attorney, you will sign a fee agreement that allows the SSA to directly pay your attorney out of the past due benefits if your claim is approved.

All SSDI attorneys must take cases on contingency. This means that the attorney only gets paid if the claim is approved.

All attorneys and non-attorney advocates charge the same amount if they win your case. Since you would be paying the same amount, either way, we recommend choosing an attorney vs. a non-attorney advocate.

What Is Back Pay & How Does It Work?

The SSA pays attorneys out of the back-pay, or the past due benefits. For example, if you become disabled on January 2, the SSA will round up to the next month (February) then add 5 months. The SSA would start putting your monthly benefits into a 'piggy-bank' beginning in July.

Every month you are waiting, the SSA is putting your benefits into the 'piggy-bank.' If you win your case the following July, your 'piggy-bank' would have approximately 12 months of your Social Security payments in it. Your attorney gets 25% of the 'piggy-bank' but no more than $6,000. This 25% with a cap of $6,000 applies if your case is won at the Application, Reconsideration, or Hearing stages.

If the case is won at the Appeals Council or in Federal Court, the $6,000 fee cap is removed, and the attorney gets a flat 25% of the 'piggy-bank.' It is important to know that if you lose at the Appeals Council and you are represented by a non-attorney advocate, you are not eligible to file an appeal in Federal Court.

There are five levels at which attorneys can charge fees based upon the stage of the application process as well as whether or not the Social Security claim is approved or not:

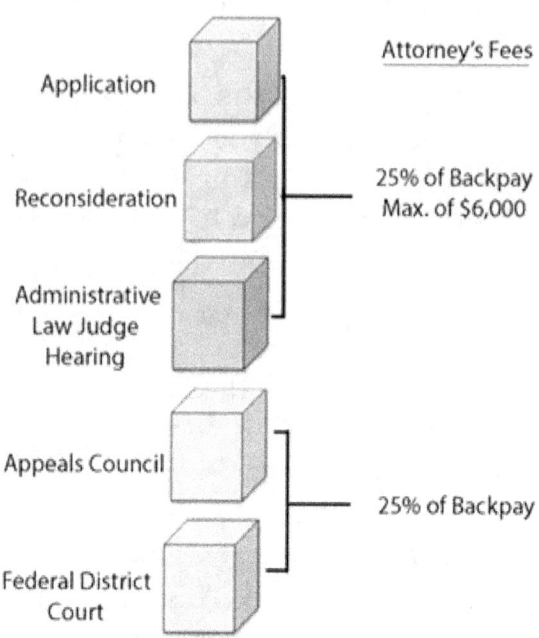

Application

Reconsideration

Administrative
Law Judge
Hearing

Appeals Council

Federal District
Court

Attorney's Fees

25% of Backpay
Max. of $6,000

25% of Backpay

*Equal Access to Justice Act Fees ("EAJA") are not included in this diagram. If an attorney wins the case in Federal Court and the SSA took an unreasonable position denying you benefits, the attorney is also entitled to EAJA fees. These fees are not paid by you. EAJA fees are paid by the government and are awarded based on an hourly rate to attorneys.

Social Security Disability: Self-Representation Lowers Chances of Approval

Applicants in Illinois may overlook one factor that raises the risk of claim denial: handling the application process alone. Observance of filing requirements and deadlines is critical in SSDI claims, and self-representing applicants often make needless mistakes. People who represent themselves do not realize that when they hire a lawyer after initially being turned down, they are going to pay the lawyer the exact same amount as if they hired the lawyer before they applied.

Initial Claim Complications

Applicants may not realize that they should supply their own medical records when filing for SSDI benefits. Applicants may believe the SSA is responsible for obtaining necessary records. However, leaving the task of gathering documentation to the SSA can lead to slower processing, and if important records are overlooked, the claim may be wrongly denied.

Applicants who work with representatives have a better understanding of the medical information they must provide. A representative can also ensure that a full range of documentation is submitted, including evaluations from treating physicians, treatment records and objective evidence, such as lab tests, biopsy results or x-rays.

The documentation provided should reflect the way the individual intends to qualify for benefits. There are various ways an SSDI applicant may establish eligibility for benefits:

- The applicant may meet requirements for an SSA impairment listing. Besides suffering from a recognized disabling condition, the individual must have symptoms or test results that meet SSA criteria.

- The applicant may receive a medical vocational allowance if he or she cannot work due to a combination of impairments.

- The applicant may also receive an allowance if he or she is deemed incapable of resuming past jobs and unfit to learn a new job, based on factors such as age, education, and employment history.

Self-representing individuals who are unfamiliar with these means of qualifying may fail to provide adequate documentation of medical and work history. These mistakes can cost an applicant time and benefits. Rather than risk claim denials, applicants are better served working with an SSD attorney who will be familiar with evidence requirements, filing deadlines and other SSA procedures.

Chapter 4

How the Social Security Administration (SSA) Decides A Case

The SSA uses what it refers to as the "5-Step Sequential Evaluation Process" to decide whether to award or deny benefits to claimants. This chapter will give a brief overview of the "5-Step Sequential Evaluation Process."

Below is a typical judge's explanation of the law and the 5-Step Sequential Evaluation Process that is required to use in determining whether or not an individual is disabled.

1. Are you working?

The first inquiry SSA makes is whether or not you are working. The SSA will look at your Certified Tax Earnings Records to see if you have been making more money each month than the limited monthly Substantial Gainful Activity ("SGA") amount for that year. If you make more money than the SGA amount, you will not be eligible for benefits.[7]

---

[7] Refer to Chapter 2 to see the SGA amount for previous years.

Note: The SSA evaluates self-employment differently than working for a business and receiving a W-2. The SSA scrutinizes self-employed individuals more so than individuals who are not self-employed. In the eyes of the SSA it is much easier for self-employed individuals to conceal money by not reporting their total income to the IRS.

2. Do You Have a Severe Medically Determinable Impairment?

A Severe Medically Determinable Impairment, according to the SSA, is an impairment or a combination of impairments that significantly limits the individual's physical or mental abilities and, as a result, interferes with the individual's ability to perform basic work activities. When the SSA looks at your disability, it is focusing on the frequency and intensity of symptoms and how they affect your ability to work.

For example, you can be diagnosed with Multiple Sclerosis (MS), be asymptomatic and run marathons, and have no functional limitations. Alternatively, you can be diagnosed with MS and be in a wheelchair.

The SSA is looking at both your diagnosis and limitations that result from your condition. Simply being diagnosed with a condition does not automatically translate to having a Severe Medically Determinable Impairment.

3. Do You Meet or Equal a Listed Impairment?

The SSA breaks down disabilities into 14 different categories. If you qualify under one of these categories, you are presumed to be disabled. The 14 categories are:

1. Musculoskeletal System
2. Special Senses and Speech
3. Respiratory Disorders
4. Cardiovascular System
5. Digestive System
6. Genitourinary Disorders
7. Hematological Disorders
8. Skin Disorders
9. Endocrine Disorders
10. Congenital Disorders that Affect Multiple Body Systems
11. Neurological Disorders
12. Mental Disorders
13. Cancer (Malignant Neoplastic Diseases)
14. Immune System Disorders[8]

The SSA uses two terms when it comes to these categories or "listings". The terms they use are "meeting a listing" and "equaling a listing." Meeting a listing means that you meet each of the criteria in the specific listing. Equaling a listing means that you do not have all of the criteria relating to the specific listing,

---

[8] To the view the list online go to:
https://www.ssa.gov/disability/professionals/bluebook/AdultListings.htm

but you have another disability that causes you to have the symptoms or limitations that equal the missing criteria of the listing.

4. Can You Do Your Past Relevant Work?

The judge will come up with a Residual Functional Capacity ("RFC"). The RFC is created (before step 4) from the testimony and medical records that have been provided, although the medical records play a larger role. The RFC is the most physical and mental activity an individual can perform despite their disabilities. This is used to determine if you can do any of your Past Relevant Work ("PRW") or any other work that exists in the national economy.

PRW is any work you have done in the last 15 years and made more than the SGA amount for the year the work was performed. The SSA will only look back at your past 15 years of work history.

If you have the RFC to do your PRW, then you are not disabled in the eyes of the SSA. If you are unable to do any of your past relevant work or do not have any PRW, the analysis proceeds to the fifth and final step.

5. Can You Do Other Jobs That Are Available?

The SSA hires Vocational Rehabilitation Experts to assist them at this step. The testimony of a vocational expert (VE) can be an invaluable tool as you set out to prove the extent and consequences of your disability.

Out of all of the people at your hearing, the VE will be the one to whom the ALJ looks for answers about your ability to go back to work. The VE will comment on what job duties he or she thinks you can perform given your disability and look at your work history to determine whether or not you can continue to successfully carry out the duties that your last job requires. If not, he or she will make recommendations on your skillset and how that can be transferred to other work opportunities.

In most cases, the judge and your attorney will then pose a number of questions to the vocational expert based on your documented disability. This portion of the hearing is to show whether or not a hypothetical person with your disability could do the job. If the answer is "yes," your claim will be denied. If the VE believes that your health condition would prevent you from going back to that particular position, he or she will then be asked if there are any other similar jobs you can do. Your attorney's role is to ask the VE follow-up questions to show that you are unable to do any relevant jobs and are, therefore, in need of disability benefits.

The VE's testimony is given a great deal of weight by your ALJ. Therefore, it is crucial that you have a Social Security attorney on your side. An experienced lawyer will understand the ins and outs of the law in order to refute any testimony the VE may have given about jobs you can still do. In addition, he or she can act as your ally as you navigate the disability claims system.

Note: This part of the hearing is often the most confusing for people who apply for benefits. The judge will be questioning the VE about individuals who are of a similar age, educational background, and work experience, along with the limitations they have.

Chapter 5

What Forms Must Be Completed During the SSDI Application Process?

Applying for Social Security Disability (SSDI) requires a lot of paperwork. Whether you apply online, over the phone, by mail, or in person at your local SSA office, there are a number of forms that must be completed in order to open an SSDI case.

Keep in mind that these forms all request similar information. It is therefore extremely important that your answers are consistent across all forms. Inconsistencies can cause delays in your application while the disability determination examiner seeks to clarify the discrepancies; they may decrease your application's credibility. Your SSDI attorney can help you complete these forms.

Application for Disability Benefits

Your SSDI case begins with the Application for Disability Insurance Benefits (Form SSA-16- BK). It asks for your personal information, including your birth and citizenship, family history, veteran and employment status, work and earnings history, and medical conditions. This checklist outlines all of the information you will need to complete the application. All documents provided must be an original or certified copy.

Adult Disability Report

A single error on just one SSD form could result in a denial of benefits. For this very reason, it is imperative that people who are applying for benefits take the time to understand how these forms should be completed, particularly the SSDI report form.

The SSA does not want any sections or lines left blank. Incomplete forms can lead to an unnecessary denial by the SSA, and it is estimated that a large portion of denials are linked to incomplete paperwork. You should go over each line carefully to ensure you have not overlooked a box or a line.

The Adult Disability Report (Form SSA-3368- BK) is an 11-page document designed to gather detailed information about your medical condition, earnings history, work history and individuals (medical and non-medical) with knowledge of your condition.
The report has several sections and asks for the following information:

- Personal information, such as date of birth and contact numbers
- Contact information for at least one individual (other than a medical provider) with knowledge of your medical condition
- Your medical condition(s)
- Work activity, including any changes you have had to make in your job due to your disability
- Education and training
- Jobs history for up to the last five jobs you've had in the 15 years before becoming unable to work
- Medication taken, including name, dose, and frequency
- Treatment received for your condition, including all doctor's and ER visits and overnight hospital stays
- Other medical information
- Remarks, which allow you to add anything else you believe is relevant to helping the SSA evaluate your eligibility

Be as detailed as possible when completing the adult disability report. The more complete and accurate the information provided is, the better the chances that your SSDI application will be approved.

Work History Report

The Work History Report (Form SSA-3369- BK) deals exclusively with your work history. If you have had more than five jobs in the 15 years before becoming disabled, you will be able to include all of this information on the Work History Report (as compared to the Adult Disability Report, which only has space for five prior jobs).

For each of your prior jobs, the Work History Report requests details about your wages, education, and job training, as well as your specific job duties and how your disability impacted your ability to complete your responsibilities. Make sure you write down the most you had to lift. Even if it was only once in a while. If it was required to do your job, like lifting a case of water if you were the office manager or moving a computer, Social Security needs to know about it. If somebody was doing the lifting for you, you need to tell this to Social Security. You also need to list all of your job duties and not just the main one. In reality, there is no job that exists where the employee does not have to lift 20 pounds.

10 Guidelines for Answering a Social Security Function Report (Form SSA-3373-BK)

Here are some guidelines for you to use when answering questions in a Social Security Function report:

Guideline 1: Tell the truth.

We tell our clients to tell the truth to the Social Security office. Take the time and pay attention to each question so you can understand what information the SS office is trying to find out. This is the SSA's one-minute look at what is going on with you.

Some Examples:

Question: Do you take care of anyone else such as a wife/husband, children, grandchildren, parents, friend, other?
Answer: We had a client answer, "yes" to this question.

Question: Who are you taking care of?
Answer: My grandmother.

Question: Where does your grandmother live?
Answer: California.

Question: How do you take care of your grandmother in California if you live in Illinois?
Answer: I pay for her nursing home care out of a trust.

Social Security assumes that when you take care of somebody, you are doing that person's cooking, cleaning, laundry, grocery shopping and other daily activities. In this case, the client gave the wrong answer.

If you have children and they help you, make sure you mention this. If your children are older, note if they help you more than you help them.

Guideline 2: Put the words "on a bad day" in front of each question.

Question: Do you prepare meals?
Answer: The answer should not just be "yes."
Be detailed about your answer. Explain the difficulties you have if applicable.

Example Answer: On a bad day, I lays in bed, and my family brings her food. On a good day, I can cook a meal in the microwave for myself.

If you were to state that you can cook, the SS office may assume that you can cook larger meals an without difficulty. So be specific!

Guideline 3: Take each question seriously, even if it may not seem important.

Questions on Personal Care

For Dressing, Example Answers:
- I need help with zippers and buttons because I have no feeling in my fingers.
- I get dressed very slowly because of the pain.
- I can't put certain types of shirts on because I can't lift my arms over my head.

- I need to take a break in the middle of getting dressed in the morning for 10 minutes because of the pain.
- I need help getting my shoes and socks on, because I can't bend over.

For Bathing, Example Answer:
- When I shower, I use a shower chair because I can't get in and out of the bathtub.
- I also can't bend over to wash myself because of my back pain.

Care for hair, Example Answers:
- I had my hair cut short because I can't use a blow dryer since it hurts my back.
- I can't stand long enough to blow dry my hair.
- I can't lift my arm up that high.
- The hair dryer is too heavy.

Shaving, Example Answer:
- I have problems holding the razor because my hands go numb.

Feeding myself, Example Answer:
- My spouse cuts my food.
- I don't eat food that needs to be cut up, because cutting food hurts my hands since I have carpal tunnel syndrome.

Using the toilet, Example Answer:
- I added a riser
- It takes me 20 minutes each time, because it is so difficult to get on and off in addition to the terrible pain

Other Personal Care Example Answers:
- I have to take my pain medicine and lay in bed for 30 minutes in the morning until the medicine works

Guideline 4: Try to figure out how the Social Security office can manipulate your answers to work against you. Could they re-word your answers to make it sound like you do not qualify for disability or that there may be another job you could qualify to do?

Examples:
If you say, "I take my dog for a walk," could you be a dog walker?

If you say, "I do the family dishes," could you be a dishwasher?

Guideline 5: Relate your functional limitation to the answer.

Guideline 6: Keep your answers short yet detailed—you don't need more space than is provided. Remember, loose links sink ships. In other words, the more you say, the more the SSA can relay what you say to a job.

Question: How do your illnesses, injuries, or conditions limit your ability to work?

- **Answer**: My Multiple Sclerosis causes me to forget information. I have lost control of my bladder, so I have to go the bathroom all the time and change my pad.

- **Answer**: My back pain limits me from lifting more than five pounds, and I can't stand for more than five minutes, so I couldn't walk to my workstation.

- **Answer**: I can't work a full day because my Crohn's Disease causes me to go to the bathroom 4 to 10 times per day for 10 to 30 minutes at a time.

Guideline 7: Use specific numbers when possible.

Examples:
- I can only lift 5 pounds
- I go to the bathroom 4 to 10 times per day

Guideline 8: Give your doctors the same answers as you have on your questionnaire. The SSA is looking to see that your doctor's records match the answers to your questionnaires.

Guideline 9: Don't volunteer any information, especially activities.

Guideline 10: Have a third party read over your answers to ensure that your answers don't suggest that you can perform more tasks than you can actually do in a work setting. Also, the third party might suggest functional limitations to include that you had not thought of.

Authorization to Disclose Information (Form SSA 827)

The Authorization to Disclose Information (Form SSA 827) grants permission to the SSA to receive and request your medical history and other confidential information. Your case cannot proceed without it.

Failure to complete and submit any of the required forms will result in your application being delayed or denied.

Chapter 6

What Can You Do to Help Your Case?

Go to the doctor!

Your doctor(s) will never be asked to testify in your disability case, but their records are the most important documents in your case. Medical records are the evidence your attorney will use to prove your case. Without this evidence, your claim will be denied.

The SSA does not care about what you or your attorney say about your condition. Likewise, the SSA does not care about what a family member or friend says in a Third-Party Function Report (Form SSA-3380-BK). The SSA is looking for objective evidence proving you cannot work. The SSA only cares about what you say to the extent that it be consistent with what your doctor says and what the objective evidence shows.

According to the SSA, "Objective medical evidence is evidence that is obtained from the application of medically acceptable clinical and laboratory diagnostic techniques, such as evidence of reduced joint motion, muscle spasm, sensory deficit or motor disruption.

Objective medical evidence of this type is a useful indicator to assist us in making reasonable conclusions about the intensity and persistence of your symptoms and the effect those symptoms, such as pain, may have on your ability to work.

We must always attempt to obtain objective medical evidence and, when it is obtained, we will consider it in reaching a conclusion as to whether you are disabled. However, we will not reject your statements about the intensity and persistence of your pain or other symptoms or about the effect your symptoms have on your ability to work solely because the available objective medical evidence does not substantiate your statements."[9]

Objective evidence is key in a disability case, and treatment that is consistent with the diagnosis is even more important. Clients often tell us about nasty falls they have taken and ask if they should tell the judge or not. If the client did not go to a hospital or tell their doctor about the fall, there will not be any concrete evidence to present to the judge.

On average, we estimate that a client's disability file is about 1,000 pages long. A large disability file is about 4,000 pages. Before a hearing, we always read and discuss our clients' medical records and speculate what the judge may ask. We explain inconsistencies in the

---

[9] § 404.1529 (B) How we evaluate symptoms, including pain. https://www.ssa.gov/OP_Home/cfr20/404/404-1529.htm

records and shed light on both the strengths and weaknesses of a case. We consistently find evidence that may hurt our clients in a hearing, including visits to the gym and attempts to do yard work. In a disability case, anything you say to your doctor can and will be used against you.

We recommend being aware of ambiguity in your records. A few months ago, we had a client approach us before her hearing and asked our thoughts on her case. Her record noted that she takes care of her elderly mother. As attorneys, we read this as ambiguous and vague. Our client told us that she pays for her mother's nursing home out of her retirement savings.

A judge may think that this statement includes chores, such as cooking, cleaning, laundry, and grocery shopping. Our client was shocked that this statement was in her records and that it could be used against her. At the hearing, we made sure to discuss this statement in full detail in front of the judge, which prevented the judge from using the statement against our client. Be cautious and detail-oriented when telling your doctor information. Current consistent medical treatment is imperative to your case, so always make sure to go to your doctor.

Have Your Doctor Complete a Medical Source Statement

One of the biggest problems with medical records is what they do not say. Medical records will often diagnose you with a condition and contain your subjective complaints. Despite all the information, medical records contain, they do not ordinarily include information regarding an applicant's functional residual capacity – what they can and cannot do because of their disability. For example, if you worked as an administrative assistant and began to experience tremors and decreased fine motor control following a stroke, MRIs and other diagnostic imaging could help prove that the stroke occurred. Medical notes may mention the tremors, and treatment notes from occupational therapists will make note of the decreased fine motor skills.

While the medical record would prove that you suffered a stroke and the effects it had on you, it does not provide any insight into the stroke's effect on your ability to work. There is no evidence of the stroke's impact on your mental focus, your ability to comprehend instructions and follow through on assigned tasks, or how your decreased fine motor skills affect your typing and filing abilities. All of these work specific limitations are what make you unable to return to work as an administrative assistant.

Without your doctor specifically stating your mental or physical limitations, the judge assigned to your case will make up the limitations based on her review of the record. More often than not, the judge's limitations will be inaccurate, and that is why you must have a medical source statement ("MSS") filled out by one or more of your treating medical providers.

An MSS is a statement from one of your medical providers, most commonly a doctor, that provides your mental or physical limitations and their impact on various work activities.

The longer the medical provider has treated you, the more credible the MSS will be. Simply seeing a doctor one time and having the doctor fill out an MSS will not be beneficial.

Your attorney should give you special MSS's for your specific conditions and treatments. If you are going to have more than one of your medical providers fill out a medical source statement, you need to make sure the MSS's are consistent between doctors. If there are inconsistencies in the MSS's, some judges will use the inconsistencies to discredit your doctors.

What Is Needed in a Medical Source Statement?

The medical source statement elicits the information necessary to help support your claim that your disability negatively affects your ability to work. An effective medical source statement should include detailed information regarding:

- Diagnosis

- Results of clinical exams

- Prescribed treatments, including dose, frequency and duration, and responses to each treatment, positive or negative

- Laboratory findings, such as blood work, X-rays, MRIs, and CT scans

- Functional capabilities and functional deficits, especially those that relate specifically to the patient's job functions, including gross and fine motor tasks and communication deficits

Without information in the file regarding the physical and mental limitations caused by the stroke, the disability examiner and medical consultants hired by the Social Security Administration—neither of whom can be considered impartial—will come to their own conclusions regarding the stroke's effect on your ability to work, even though they may have never met or examined you.

In addition to supporting your SSDI application, completing a medical source statement reduces the chance that your SSDI attorney will need to subpoena your doctors, should the case proceed to an administrative hearing. Administrative law judges place great weight on medical source statements completed by your treating physician, so it is important that they be completed as accurately as possible and with as much information as possible.

One of the services our office provides is the correct preparation and gathering of medical documentation. Our office has prepared medical source statements specific to more than 100 disabling conditions for your physician to complete. These forms are designed to elicit the information needed to help the SSA accurately assess your functional residual capacity and determine your ability to return to your prior work or perform some other work suitable for your age, skill set, and educational background.

What Is an Acceptable Medical Source? (AMS)

Medical evidence plays a huge role in determining the outcome of SSD claims. In 2010, just over half of all SSDI claim denials at the initial level were made on a medical basis, according to a report from the SSA.. The SSA has established strict standards for medical evidence, including the use of acceptable medical sources. SSDI applicants in Illinois risk claim denial if they fail to provide adequate evidence from an acceptable medical source (AMS).

The following are AMS's:
- Licensed physicians (medical or osteopathic doctors)

- Licensed or certified psychologists at the independent practice level

- School psychologists, or other licensed or certified individuals with other titles who perform the same function as a school psychologist in a school setting, are AMSs for impairments of intellectual disability, learning disabilities, and borderline intellectual functioning only

- Licensed optometrists for impairments of visual disorders, or measurement of visual acuity and visual fields only, depending on the scope of practice in the State in which the optometrist practices

- Licensed podiatrists for impairments of the foot, or foot and ankle only, depending on whether the State in which the podiatrist practices permits the practice of podiatry on the foot only, or the foot and ankle

- Qualified speech-language pathologists (SLPs) for speech or language impairments only. For this source, "qualified" means that the SLP must be licensed by the State professional licensing agency, or be fully certified by the State education agency in the State that he or she practices, or hold a Certificate of Clinical

Competence in Speech-Language-Pathology from the American Speech-Language Hearing Association

- In claims with a filing date on or after March 27, 2017, licensed physician assistants for impairments within the licensed scope of practice only

- In claims with a filing date on or after March 27, 2017, licensed audiologists for impairments of hearing loss, auditory processing disorders, and balance disorders within the licensed scope of practice only

  - **NOTE:** Audiologists' scope of practice generally includes evaluation, examination, and treatment of certain balance impairments that result from the audio-vestibular system. However, some impairments involving balance involve several different body systems that are outside the scope of practice for audiologists, such as those involving muscles, bones, joints, vision, nerves, heart and blood vessels

- In claims with a filing date on or after March 27, 2017, licensed Advanced Practice Registered Nurses (APRN), also known in some States as Advanced Practice Nurse (APN), and Advanced Registered Nurse Practitioner (ARNP) for impairments within his or her licensed scope of practice

There are four types of APRNs with a handful of State variations:

1. Certified Nurse Midwife (CNM);
2. Nurse Practitioner (NP);
3. Certified Registered Nurse Anesthetist (CRNA); and
4. Clinical Nurse Specialist (CNS).

Accepted Sources

The SSA requires that acceptable medical sources do the following:

- Officially diagnose the disabling condition
- Provide medical opinions on the prognosis, severity, and effects of the disability or illness
- Act as the applicant's treating source

Treatment and evidence from other medical sources is not necessarily inadmissible in an SSDI claim. The SSA acknowledges that managed healthcare has resulted in more individuals seeking medical treatment from professionals who are not acceptable medical sources. The SSA recognizes the validity of objective evidence from these sources, such as medical imaging. Professional opinions from these other medical professionals also can bolster an SSDI applicant's claim.

Supporting Evidence

Evidence from other medical sources, such as physician assistants or nurse practitioners, can help establish the severity of a condition and the resulting functional limitations. When weighing this evidence and its accuracy, an SSA claims examiner considers whether or not the medical source has a history of treating the applicant and specializes in a relevant field. The examiner also evaluates whether or not the source's observations or opinions are consistent with the other medical evidence.

To review all relevant medical evidence when considering an applicant's impairments, the SSA also considers evidence from non-medical sources. These sources include people who have treated the applicant in a professional capacity, such as social workers and counselors. People who have non-working relationships with the applicant, such as family members and friends, can also act as non-medical sources.

Tell Your Doctor the Numbers

The numbers relevant to your case include the following:

- How long you can sit
- How long you can stand
- How far you can walk
- How much you can carry

- How much you can lift
- How much you can push
- How much you can pull
- How long you can focus
- How many breaks you would need during a work day and how long the breaks would be
- How much of a work day could you use your hands
- How much of the workday could you reach overhead

When you are diagnosed with a disabling impairment, your medical providers will take notes about how they reached their conclusion. Most often it will be through testing and explanation of your subjective symptoms but sometimes, the specific numbers are left out of the files.

Where there are no specifically defined limitations and numbers, the judge or consultative medical examiner will substitute his opinion for what they think your doctor would have written. The judges and consultative medical examiner are not your treating physician. Moreover, they have never met you and are likely unaware of a lot of pertinent information related to your specific case. Your medical records are often thousands of pages long. Despite the length of your records, if the specific limitations and numbers are left out, you are left at the mercy of the judge and/or consultative medical examiner's interpretation of your records.

Anything You Say Can and Will Be Used Against You!

The phrase, "Anything you say can and will be used against you in a court of law" traditionally applies only in criminal cases, but individuals applying for disability should also keep this phrase in mind. Below are some scenarios where an applicant's words can be used against him:

Think Twice Before Going to a Social Security Administration Field Office

If an applicant goes into a Social Security Administration ("SSA") field office, the employees there may take field observations of you. These field observations are typically about an applicant's appearance and behavior. If your appearance or behavior is inconsistent with the disabilities you have alleged, your responses to questionnaires sent to you by the SSA, or statements doctors have made in your medical records, it can be used against you. If you do not go into an SSA field office, they cannot take field observations that may later be used against you. We recommend avoiding all SSA field offices unless it is completely necessary. A willing friend or family member can go in your place.

What You Tell Your Doctors and Medical Providers Can Be Used Against You

As stated before, medical records are the most important component of any Social Security Disability case. At all levels of the disability process, medical records are reviewed and read by SSA employees. Doctors are often rushing to take notes that ultimately end up in your medical records, and these rushed notes taken by doctors can and will be used against you. If at a doctor's appointment you tell your doctor you are having a good day, it will be in your records.

If on your next several visits you tell your doctor you are having a bad day, it will be noted in your medical records, as well. It is natural for even the sickest people to have good and bad days. While ALJ's certainly tend to overemphasize the good ones, there's also a good argument to be made that someone who always has a bad day is exaggerating. The best advice on this point would be to be honest, but recognize the pitfalls of saying you're fine just to be polite.

Be Careful of What You, Your Friends, and Your Family Say in Social Security's Questionnaires and Third-Party Function Reports

When you apply for Social Security Disability benefits, credibility is a significant factor that the SSA considers. The statements that you make about your ability to care for your personal needs, including your ability to cook, clean, do laundry, and grocery shop, matter. If a family or friend reports anything differently than you do in a Third-Party Function Report, the SSA will surely use those inconsistencies against you.

Chapter 7

Hearings: Who, What, Where, When, and Why?

Who?

At a Social Security Disability hearing, the following people are present:

- The claimant (the person who applied)
- The claimant's attorney
- The Administrative Law Judge (ALJ)
- A hearing monitor who records the audio
- A vocational expert who testifies about the claimant's work that may or may not be available to the claimant
- In some cases, a medical expert will be brought in to testify about the claimant's physical or mental impairments

What?

At most Social Security Disability hearings, the Administrative Law Judge (ALJ) will first introduce himself/herself and state where the hearing is being held. If you have a representative, the ALJ will ask you if you have gone over the fee agreement and appointment of representation (SSA forms: 1696 & 827). Then, the ALJ will ask you, and any expert witnesses present, to take an oath and to tell the truth.

During the majority of the hearings, the ALJ will pose most of the questions to the claimant, but in some instances, the ALJ will have the attorney ask the questions instead.

Some of the more common questions you may be asked are listed below. If you are appearing at a disability hearing, you can expect additional questions. ALJs and attorneys ask these questions to determine whether or not you are disabled under Social Security's very specific definition of disability.

Common Questions Asked by the ALJ at a Hearing:

- When did you start working?
- Who do you live with?
- What is preventing you from working?
- Why does your medical impairment prevent you from working?
- How long have you suffered from your medical impairment?
- How did your last job end? (i.e., Were you fired? Did you quit?)
- Is there any job you think you can do?
- How long can you sit/stand/walk?

- Do you have trouble lifting yourself from a sitting to a standing position?
- How much can you lift/carry?
- How many hours do you sleep per night?
- Do you take naps?
- Can you describe a typical day and what you do from the time you wake up until the time you go to sleep?
- Who does the cooking at home?
- Who does the cleaning at home?
- Who does the grocery shopping at home?
- What kind of home do you live in? (i.e., condo, Apt. house, etc.)
- Are there stairs to enter your home?
- Are there stairs inside your home?

When you see the doctor, he or she will write down the parts of your conversation that will be in your medical records. ALJs will compare the statements you make at your SSDI hearing with the statements you have made to your doctors. They will also compare the statements you make at your hearing with any questionnaires you have completed and any third-party function reports that were completed by friends, family, and former co-workers and the notes contained in your medical records. It is of the utmost importance that all information in your record is consistent.

Where?

SSD hearings are held at the various Offices of Disability Adjudication and Review (O.D.A.R.). Many of the hearing office are nestled away in office buildings and cannot be seen from the street.

Below is the current list of Offices of Disability Adjudication and Review locations in Illinois as of 2018:

Chicago:
Citadel Building
131 S. Dearborn, 25th Floor
Chicago, IL 60603

Evanston:
Northwestern University Research Park
1033 University Place, Suite 200
Evanston, IL 60201

NHC Chicago:
200 West Adams, 15th Floor
Chicago, IL 60606

Orland Park:
15401 South 94th Avenue
Orland Park, IL 60462

Peoria:
3328 W. Willow Knolls Drive

Peoria, IL 61614

<u>Oak Brook</u>:
2301 West 22nd Street, Suite 201
Oak Brook, IL 60523

When?

Hearings are the third step in the Social Security
Disability process. As of 2017, it typically takes more
than two years from the day you apply to the day you
get your actual hearing.

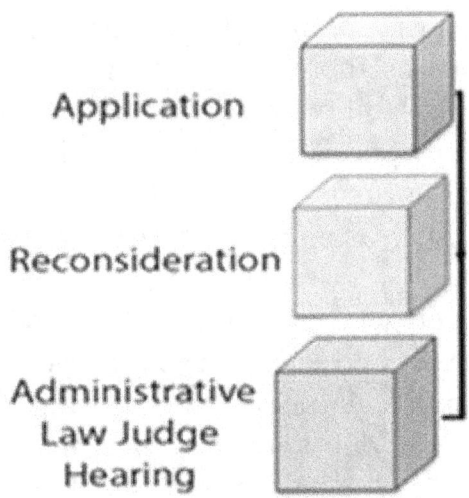

While some might imagine a Social Security Disability hearing as being a formal proceeding in a large courtroom, applicants for Social Security Disability benefits may be surprised to learn that the process is actually quite informal and very different from that of a regular trial hearing.

Most Social Security Disability hearings are held at the applicant's local Social Security hearing office. However, if the applicant lives far from the hearing office, the hearing may take place in a conference room at a hotel or may even be held by the use of video conferencing software.

Since the hearing is informal, applicants also do not have to dress as though they are at a regular court appearance. Disability lawyers often ask their clients to dress for their Social Security Disability hearings as they would normally dress, of course with some restrictions, such as no hats or revealing clothing.

TIP: When you get paperwork for Social Security, fill it out immediately and send it to your lawyer to review so he or she can submit it. Social Security will give you 14-60 days to fill out and send in your documents. Waiting to fill out your documents will ultimately add to the amount of time it will take you to get a hearing.

Why?

Social Security hearings are meant to give claimants the opportunity to present their case. A Social Security Disability hearing has a routine cast of characters applicants will see – the ALJ, Social Security Disability lawyers, a vocational expert, and a court reporter.

The hearing will be presided over by an ALJ. The applicant's SSD lawyer will also be present to advocate on behalf of the applicant. A vocational expert is available to give insight into the applicant's line of work. A hearing monitor is present to record what happens in the hearing.

First, the court reporter will swear in the applicant, the vocational expert, and any witnesses to the hearing. Then the ALJ asks the vocational expert hypothetical questions about what kind of jobs a person with the applicant's limitations could perform. The ALJ may also invite the applicant to speak and describe their limitations and how they are prevented from working. The ALJ will be comparing the applicant's statements to the medical records to see if the testimony is consistent throughout.

Typically, these SSD hearings are quite short and can last anywhere from 15 minutes to an hour. Because the hearings are short, it is very important that applicants be on time as ALJs have busy schedules. An ALJ may refuse to have a hearing for an applicant who is late if his schedule is packed for the day. As a rule of thumb, it is a good idea to arrive at least 45 minutes before the hearing.

After the SSSD hearing takes place, the applicant's file remains at the hearing office until the ALJ makes a decision on the case. When the ALJ is ready, he or she will either deny or approve the award of SSD benefits.

If the claim is denied, the applicant's file will remain at the hearing office in case the applicant chooses to appeal the ALJ's decision. A notice of denial is sent to the applicant and his attorney or representative? with instructions on how to appeal the decision.

If the claim is approved, a Social Security representative will confirm the applicant's income eligibility, and will then send a notice of award letter to the applicant informing him or her that the judge approved their benefits. This letter explains how much the benefits will be and when the applicant can expect to receive them.

Chapter 8

Why Claims Are Denied & What You Can Do?

The chances of having an application for Social Security Disability or Supplemental Security Income approved are low. SSDI and SSI have quite similar names, but these government programs have substantial differences. Supplemental Security Income (SSI) and Social Security Disability Insurance (SSDI) are two distinctive programs and it is important for potential applicants to know the distinction between the two and how these affect the outcome of an application.

You Do Not Have the Work Credits for SSDI

SSDI is a benefit that applicants earn and it is financed by the Social Security taxes that are paid by workers and employers. As a result, SSDI benefits are based on an applicant's work record, just like retirement benefits, and are not considered to be welfare. In order to qualify for Social Security Disability (SSDI) benefits, applicants must have worked long enough to reach insured status with the Social Security Administration (SSA). To reach this status, you must have worked long enough during your career to contribute a certain amount to the Social Security system through taxes deducted from your paychecks. The SSA uses a system of "work credits" to determine whether you have obtained this minimum level of contribution and whether you qualify for SSDI.

The SSA decides whether you have worked long enough to qualify for SSDI benefits by converting your job earnings into work credits. This amount is calculated annually and is accumulated over the course of a person's career. When you work and pay your Social Security taxes, you can earn up to four work credits each year.

The amount of earnings it takes to earn a work credit changes over time. Credits are also based on your total wages and income during the year, no matter when you performed the actual work. Therefore, you could earn your work credits for the year in a short time.

In 2018, you must earn $1,320 to earn one credit, or $5,080 to earn the maximum amount of work credits for the year. As a result, it does not take a high amount of earnings to receive credit for a year of paying into the Social Security system. What matters even more for SSDI eligibility is how many years you have worked.

The number of work credits needed for SSDI benefits depends on the age you were when you became disabled. Generally, applicants need 40 work credits, 20 of which were earned in the last 10 years ending in the year the applicant became disabled. However, younger disabled workers may qualify for SSDI with fewer work credits.

Keep these general rules in mind:

- Before age 24 – you may qualify for SSDI benefits if you earned 6 credits in the 3-year period ending when your disability starts
- Age 24 to 31 – you may qualify for SSDI benefits if you have credit for working half the time between age 21 and the time you become disabled
- Age 31 or older – generally, you need to have the number of work credits shown in the chart below.

Born after 1929, Became Disabled At This Age	Number of Work Credits Needed
31 through 42	20
44	22
46	24
48	26
50	28
52	30
54	32
56	34
58	36
60	38
62 or older	40

If you have not worked long enough to qualify for SSDI benefits, you may still be eligible for assistance through the Supplemental Security Income (SSI) program. While the SSI program does not have a work requirement, you must still be able to demonstrate financial need.

You Do Not Meet the Duration Requirement

SSDI's focus is on providing assistance to applicants with physical impairments that are so severe as to prevent those persons from otherwise engaging in normal work. For a physical deficiency to be considered severe enough to qualify for SSDI, it must be considered as having the potential to last at least 12 months or end in the applicant's death. So, if the SSA does not think an applicant's disabilities will last 12 months or end in the applicant's death the application may be denied.

You Do Not Have Enough Evidence

A successful SSDI application needs sufficient medical evidence to support its claim that the applicant is significantly affected by a disability. By learning more about what medical evidence the Social Security Administration (SSA) likes to see in applications, you can prepare your medical evidence for your SSDI application to succeed.

Timely, accurate, and adequate medical records can speed up the time it takes for the SSA to make a decision on your application. Timely records that are relevant to the applicant's current condition have great weight with disability examiners – especially if the disability is rapidly changing and requires up-to-date information. Accurate records correctly describe the applicant's disability and follow the SSA's requirements for acceptable medical sources. Adequate records contain enough information for the disability examiner to make a decision.

By including sufficient medical evidence with an SSDI application, the disability examiner has what he or she needs to make a decision and can make that decision faster as a result. Otherwise, the disability examiner would be forced to track down more medical information before he or she could make a decision on the application.

SSDI benefits are only awarded to persons who are unable to earn a livable wage due to a severe physical or mental impairment. Because of this requirement, medical evidence is the heart of any Social Security Disability Insurance (SSDI) application. Disability examiners reviewing SSDI applications determine whether a claimant qualifies for benefits by reviewing the claimant's medical records. In making this determination, the focus is not just whether the claimant is impaired, but whether his or her impairment is severe enough to prevent the claimant from earning a living. Failure to have the requisite evidence is one of the most common reasons the SSA denies initial applications.

Your SSI Application Was Denied Because You Do Not Meet the Asset Requirements

As previously discussed, SSI is a needs based program that is funded by the government and is financed by the general revenues of the U.S. Treasury Department. SSI pays benefits to low-income people at the age of 65 or older, to disabled or blind adults, and disabled or blind children. However, because of its strict financial requirements, SSI is only available to persons with limited assets and income. Therefore, if you or your loved one has more than $2,000 in assets, excluding their home and car they will be denied SSI.

Other Sources of Income and Assistance to Keep in Mind That May Affect SSDI Payments

Social Security Disability benefits are only awarded to people with income below a certain threshold. As an example, for 2014, the monthly income limit is $1,070. However, work earnings are not the only income the SSA considers when awarding SSDI benefits. Various benefits and forms of assistance can also affect SSDI eligibility and payment amounts.

Benefits awarded based on injury or disablement can affect SSDI awards. People who receive workers' compensation benefits or public disability benefits, including any lump sum settlements, will receive a reduced SSDI payment as long as the other benefits continue. Public disability benefits are any federal, state or local government awards to provide support for disabilities that are not job-related. These benefits include: Civil service disability; State temporary disability; State or local government benefits for retirement due to disability. Collectively, workers' compensation benefits, public disability benefits and SSD benefits cannot exceed 80 percent of an individual's current average earnings. However, once other benefits stop or the benefit recipient turns 65, SSDI payments will increase to the full amount.

It is crucial for individuals who receive SSDI benefits to report other disability benefits and changes in benefit amounts, including the cessation of payments, to the SSA. This ensures that recipients do not miss due payments or receive overpayments that will need to be balanced later.

There are a few forms of public income or support that do not affect SSDI payments. Veterans Administration(VA) benefits and SSI payments will not reduce SSDI benefits. People who receive state or local government benefits may also qualify for full SSDI payments, assuming these individuals have paid Social Security taxes. If your application has been denied at any stage in the process it is always best to appeal instead of reapplying.

Chapter 9

The Appeals Process

Most people who apply for Social Security Disability (SSDI) benefits will be denied on their initial application. However, receiving an initial denial is not the end of the road for people in need of disability benefits. Applicants can appeal the Social Security Administration's denials of their applications in hopes of ultimately receiving benefits.

While the appeals process can provide denied applicants with another chance, the appeals process can be lengthy. It takes getting through two levels of the appeals process before an applicant can get a hearing in front of an ALJ. Sometimes it can take up to a year or more to receive a hearing date.

Hearing Before Administrative Law Judge
Applicants waiting for their day in court before an ALJ can be prepared for their appeal by following these five tips.

1.   Gather Updated Medical Records

Having up-to-date medical evidence at your hearing is crucial in order to properly prepare for an appeal. It is imperative that you have all your most recent medical records so that a gap does not exist in your documentation.

Applicants must collect updated medical records, because the SSA will not gather additional records on your behalf before your hearing. While a disability examiner will obtain recent medical records when he or she first evaluates your claim, the development of your case typically stops when the appeal process begins.

As a result, your file could sit unchanged until an ALJ reviews your records at the hearing stage. If you have not gathered updated medical records, the information in your file may not be current enough for an ALJ to grant you disability benefits.

2.   Get a Statement from Your Doctor

A very useful piece of medical evidence for your appeal is your doctor's opinion. Ask your doctor, who has treated you in the past, to provide a supportive statement for your application. Having a detailed letter from your doctor that explains how your disability affects you and limits you can make a positive impact on your case.

3. Document Your Medical Condition

Keeping a diary of your symptoms and limitations can be very helpful in the appeals process. This is because the success of your case will depend in part on how well you testify regarding your disability. While you may remember the limitations, you experience in your daily routine, it may be harder for you to recall detailed facts about the variety of symptoms you have experienced over time. Having this record to review will improve the quality and accuracy of your testimony.

4. Review Your Case File

Before you go to your appeal hearing, you are allowed to request your entire case file from the SSA. Take the time to review your file to see if there are any missing medical records or if you notice any mistakes in the reasoning behind why the disability examiner initially denied your claim. Reviewing your case file will also help you develop arguments about why you think the examiner was wrong to deny you benefits.

5. Consider Hiring an Experienced Disability Attorney

While you are not required to hire an attorney to help you during the appeals process, working with an experienced disability attorney greatly improves your chances of winning benefits. Statistics show that applicants who are represented by attorneys at the hearing level are two times more likely to be approved for disability benefits than unrepresented applicants.

The Appeals Council

After a claimant's application is denied by an ALJ, the claimant has 60 days to file an appeal with the Appeals Council[10]. The Appeals Council may decide to hear the applicant's appeal, or it has the option to refuse to hear it at all. If the Appeals Council declines to hear the claimant's appeal, he or she may appeal the case directly to the federal court.

The Appeals Council itself is made up of over 70 ALJs.. When the Appeals Council takes an appeal, they review the claimant's case and consider all the evidence of record from the hearing with the ALJ. The Appeals Council will only reconsider decisions made by an ALJ when it is clear that the evidence that was available at the hearing did not support the ALJ's decision or if the ALJ made a procedural error.

As a result, for the Appeals Council to overturn an ALJ's decision, it must find clear-cut evidence that the ALJ's decision was incorrect. If it is determined that the ALJ acted in error, the Appeals Council will reconsider the claimant's case. In doing so, the Appeals Council will review the original evidence, as well as any

---

[10] https://www.socialsecurity.gov/appeals/appeals_process.html

additional evidence from the claimant and the ALJ's findings.

After reviewing the claimant's case, the Appeals Council can uphold, change, or reverse the ALJ's original decision. The Appeals Council may send the case back to the ALJ to reconsider his or her original decision, or the Appeals Council may decide the case on their own. The claimant is kept informed by the Council, no matter the Appeals Council's decision.

What's the Difference Between the Appeals Council and an ALJ?

While a hearing with an ALJ and review by the Appeals Council may seem similar, there are some notable differences between the two. In a hearing before an ALJ, there is only one ALJ reviewing the claimant's application and making a decision. During a review by the Appeals Council, there are multiple ALJs working together to make a decision. In addition, a hearing before an ALJ is the only place you will have an opportunity to testify under oath. The Appeals Council may review the testimony along with the ALJ's decision.

The time it takes to complete review of a claimant's case also differs greatly between a hearing with an ALJ and a review by the Appeals Council. While the time it takes for an ALJ to make a decision varies from case to case, claimants can typically expect to receive a decision in writing from the ALJ 60 to 90 days after hearing. On the other hand, the Appeals Council review process can be quite lengthy. Across the nation, the average processing time for Appeals Council review is 345 days.

Should I Appeal to an Appeals Council?

There are advantages and disadvantages for claimants to consider before deciding to move their appeal forward to the Appeals Council stage. At the Appeals Council stage, 86 percent of requests for review are denied, according to the SSA. Of the cases that are reviewed by the Appeals Council, 13 percent are remanded to the ALJ, and only 1 percent of the requested cases result in the Council issuing a new favorable decision.

While that may seem discouraging, most cases that are sent back to an ALJ are ultimately awarded disability benefits. If the review is denied, the claimant can automatically move forward with his or her appeal to federal court, where chances of receiving disability benefits are much higher.

The Federal Courts

Appealing a denial of Social Security Disability (SSDI) can be a long and stressful process. There are many levels of the appeals process, and after experiencing multiple denials, applicants may feel like they are out of options. However, the last step in the appeals process is where disability applicants are usually awarded benefits. Before giving up on your case, consider appealing your denial to a Federal District Court.

How to Appeal Your SSDI Case to Federal Court

Once you receive a denial from the Appeals Council, you have 60 days to appeal the decision in Federal Court. This is done by filing a lawsuit in your local United States District Court. The lawsuit is initiated when you submit a complaint with the court. This complaint outlines the facts in your case.

The lawsuit will be filed against the current Social Security commissioner, due to federal law. Applicants can either file a complaint themselves or hire an experienced SSDI attorney to help them with their case.

What Happens After a Lawsuit is Filed?

After the lawsuit is filed, the Court will issue a summons, which requires the SSA to show up in court for the proceedings. You must serve the summons and a copy of the complaint to the SSA at one of its Offices of the General Council ("OGC"). Take your summons and complaint to your local OGC.

Once the SSA has been served, a lawyer from the SSA will file an answer to your complaint. The answer explains why the SSA denied your claim for benefits.

Do I Have to File an Opening Brief?

After the SSA files the administrative record, which acts as their answer to the complaint, your attorney will need to file an opening brief. It is very important to hire a disability attorney who is experienced in writing federal briefs for disability benefit denials. The opening brief explains your position to the Court and why you deserve SSDI benefits.

A case for benefits can be won or lost based on an opening brief, which analyzes the ALJ's decision to deny you benefits in light of medical evidence and testimony.

The opening brief's purpose is to persuade the federal judge that the ALJ failed to properly consider the medical evidence or failed to follow the law in making his or her decision, so you should be awarded SSDI benefits.

What Happens After I File My Opening Brief?

After you file your opening brief, the SSA will have the opportunity to file a Response Brief. This is what the SSA uses to defend the ALJ's decision to deny you disability benefits to the court. Once the SSA files its Response Brief, you will have the opportunity to file a

Reply Brief, which is your last chance to tell the Court that you should have been awarded disability benefits.

After the parties have filed all of the relevant briefs, the Court can request oral arguments, though it is a rare occurrence. These are in-person arguments where each side has a chance to talk to the judge about the case. The attorney will do the talking at an oral argument, not the client.

How Will the Federal Judge Decide My Case?

The federal judge will make his or her decision based on the information received in the briefs and the oral arguments. This process can sometimes take a year.

The judge will usually do one of the following: Remand the case to a lower level of the process for reconsideration; affirm the ALJ's decision denying you disability benefits, or reverse the ALJ's decision and grant you disability benefits.

Should I File a Federal Appeal?

The thought of taking your case to federal court can seem overwhelming, especially to those who have not had much experience in a courtroom. The Federal Appeals process is used by less than one percent of disability applicants. However, it has the highest rate of success for applicants in the SSDI Appeals process. National statistics indicate that 40 percent of disability cases taken to the Federal Appeals level are eventually approved. Taking your case all the way to the Federal Appeals level could be worth your time and effort.

Keep in mind, however, two important things. First, the federal court stage of appeals may cost you money, as there are filing fees with the court system to file a civil suit. Second, the federal appeals process can be lengthy as civil suits take time and federal judges have very heavy workloads. As a result, it can take up to a year or more to receive a decision regarding your appeal. As in any level of the SSD application and approval process, legal representation is helpful and crucial.

Chapter 10

What Can You Expect After You Win Your SSDI Case?

You have received notice that you've won your SSDI case and are entitled to Social Security Disability benefits. Congratulations! Although the hard part is over, that doesn't mean you no longer have to deal with the SSA. Here is what you can expect after winning your SSDI case:

Notice of Award

Once your application is approved, the SSA will mail you a notice of award. The notice will give your monthly benefit amount, your disability onset date (the date the SSA determined you became disabled), and the date you can expect to receive payment. No SSDI payments are made until an applicant has been disabled for five months, so the earliest you should expect to receive payment is the sixth month following your disability onset date. If you qualify for SSI, the SSA will pay your SSI for the first 5 months.

If your application was approved following an appeal at the administrative hearing or appeals council levels, you will receive a separate decision notice informing you whether or not your SSDI case was approved or denied; the notice of award will be sent in a separate follow-up letter.

Continuing Disability Review ("CDR")

The SSA routinely conducts Continuing Disability Reviews (CDRs) on recipients of SSD benefits. The purpose of the CDR is to determine whether you are still eligible for benefits. How frequently your case will be subject to CDRs depends on the nature and severity of your disability, along with the likelihood of improvement, although certain situations – such as a return to work or an improvement in your medical condition – could trigger an earlier review.

When you receive a notice that the SSA will conduct a CDR, don't panic; it doesn't necessarily mean that your benefits are in danger of ending. In fact, far from it; more than 90% of applicants who undergo a CDR are approved for continued benefits. Having a basic understanding of how CDRs work, and what information you will be expected to provide, can help increase those odds.

Frequency of Continuing Disability Reviews

Once you are approved for benefits, your case will be placed in one of three categories, based on how likely the SSA expects your medical condition to improve; the SSA will notify you which category your case was placed in when it sends out the notice of award. Those categories determine the frequency of your CDRs. These categories are:

- **Medical Improvement Expected (MIE):** Once every 6 to 18 months
- **Medical Improvement Possible (MIP):** Once every three years
- **Medical Improvement Not Expected (MINE):** Once every seven, but no more once every five years

Completing the Continuing Disability Review Forms

The SSA has the burden of proving that you are no longer disabled. To make that determination, it will request and review updated medical information. The SSA can only discontinue benefits if the review finds that:

1. The severity of your disability has significantly decreased, in relation to your ability to work, or;

2. The claims examiner or a vocational specialist determines that you are capable of engaging in SGA

The SSA will mail you Form SSA-455, the Disability Update Report, when you are due for a CDR. The report usually requests information for the previous 24 months, but the timeframe could be shorter – the SSA will tell you the exact time frame the report covers. The report asks for information regarding:

- Your work history and monthly earnings;
- Whether you have the ability to return to work;
- Any improvement regarding your medical condition, and;

- Whether you have been hospitalized or visited a doctor for any type of treatment, and the reason for such visits.

One note about Form 455: Be wary of section 2, which asks for a third-party reference who knows about your medical condition and can help with the review. If the SSA denies benefits following the review and your appeal, it is rare that the information provided by a third-party will help your case. If you can't avoid putting down a name, you should only list a family member or a friend with whom you interact daily. Why? A friend you see occasionally is likely to see you on your "good" days, so any information he provides will make it appear that your medical condition is better than it actually is.

The Disability Update Report must be completed and returned within 30 days of receipt, or you risk your benefits being terminated. The SSA must notify you within 90 days that your benefits will continue, or if you must submit to a full medical review; in the case of the latter, they will send you Form SSA-454, the Continuing Disability Review Report.

Form 454 is similar to the initial benefits application, in that it requests detailed information regarding your medical history, names of all treating physicians and hospitals, and updated medical records since the date of your last case review. The SSA will request these records from the physicians and hospitals, but you can speed up the process by submitting them with the report.

Although extensive, the form is straightforward. However, following these tips can help increase the already considerable odds that your benefits will be continued:

- When completing section 3 regarding your medical condition, list the condition or conditions that led to the finding of your disability first. Then list any medical conditions that have arisen since the last CDR (or when your application was approved if this is your first CDR).

- The same goes for completing section 4 regarding medical treatment. Start with the treatment associated with the underlying disability, followed by the treatment for any new medical conditions.

- When completing section 9, which asks you to describe your day and asks whether you have trouble with certain tasks, answer the questions in terms of your worst day. Be as detailed as possible when explaining any 'Yes' answers, using numbers to detail frequency as opposed to vague terms; for example, rather than stating, "I often have difficulty getting dressed," write, "5 out of every 7 mornings, it takes me 20 minutes to put on undergarments, a shirt, pants, shoes, and socks."

Although the CDR process can be scary and intimidating, remember – more than 90% of cases are approved for continued benefits. To help ease your worries even more, our office can help you complete and submit your Form 454; you pay us a retainer, which we keep only if your benefits are continued.

Social Security Disability Back Pay

The majority of SSDI applications take more than five months to be approved. Often, though an applicant was found eligible to receive benefits, he was not receiving them because the SSA had not yet approved his application. In these cases, you are entitled to receive SSD back pay for those "lost" months of benefits. The amount of SSDI back pay you are eligible to receive depends on the date your application was submitted, your disability onset date and the date your application was approved.

You may also be entitled to receive retroactive benefits for the period before your application date if you can prove that your disability onset date occurred before your application date.

Payment of Attorney's Fees

SSDI cases are handled on a contingency basis, meaning your attorney does not receive payment unless they win your case. The SSA rules state that SSDI attorney fees may be no more than one fourth of any back pay an applicant receives, or $6,000— whichever is less.

These rules regarding attorney's fees do not include payment for incidental expenses that the attorney incurs while representing you, some of which may include phone calls, photocopying, and travel. Talk to your SSDI attorney about what charges, if any, you will be responsible for before signing a representation agreement.

Can You Work Part-Time and Receive SSDI Benefits?

Whether you need the extra income, derive some amount of pleasure or a sense of self-worth from working, or simply need a diversion that gets you out of the house, recipients of SSD benefits or SSI benefits can work part-time and still receive SSDI benefits. However, there are certain rules that must be followed to ensure continued eligibility to receive SSDI benefits.

SSDI Benefits and Substantial Gainful Activity

Social Security Disability Insurance (SSDI) benefits are paid to applicants whose disability makes them unable to engage in substantial gainful activity. During any period that you are receiving SSDI—including the period when your application is pending—you may continue to work, so long as your earnings do not exceed the level at which the SSA considers them to be substantial. In 2016, earnings of more than $1,130 per month ($1,820 if you are blind) are considered substantial and will end the receipt of benefits; the earnings amount usually changes each year.

When considering whether or not your monthly earnings are substantial, the SSA deducts any work-related expenses from your income. These work-related expenses include the cost of any item or service necessary to allow you to work due to your disability, even if these services are useful to your everyday life. Examples of deductible work-related expenses include:

- Prescription co-payments
- Counseling services
- Certain expenses for transportation to and from work
- Personal attendant
- Job coach
- Wheelchair
- Any other specialized equipment

If your net earnings, once allowable expenses are deducted, are less than what the SSA considers substantial, you will continue to receive your SSDI benefits.

Trial Work Period (TWP) and SSDI Benefits

For SSDI recipients who want to return to work, but are unsure if their disability continues to negatively impact their ability to do so, the SSA offers a trial work period ("TWP"). You may begin a TWP either during the first month you are entitled to receive benefits or the month the application for benefits was filed—whichever comes later.

During a TWP, SSDI recipients may earn an unlimited amount of income each month for nine months and still receive their full SSDI benefits. The nine months do not need to be consecutive and run over a 60-month (five-year) period. The SSA will consider an SSDI recipient to be engaged in a TWP if his or her earnings exceed $810 a month (the amount may change annually). A self-employed individual will be considered engaged in a TWP if his or her monthly earnings (less business expenses) exceed $810, or if he or she works more than 80 hours in their business.

When the TWP ends, an individual will remain eligible to receive SSDI benefits while working for the next 36 months (three years), so long as her monthly earnings do not exceed the Substantial Gainful Activity threshold.

SSI Benefits and Part-Time Work

SSI recipients may work and still receive benefits so long as their monthly earnings do not exceed the SSA's income level, which is $733 for 2016. Keep in mind that certain types of income are excluded from the SSA's calculation of your monthly income, so it may be possible for you to earn more each month and remain eligible for SSI benefits. There is no trial work period for SSI recipients.

Reporting Requirements While Working

It is important to keep the SSA informed of any work you perform while receiving benefits. You must report to the SSA whenever you:

- Start or stop work
- Have a change in your duties, hours or wages
- Start paying work-related expenses as a result of your disability

Duty to Report

You must immediately report any information to the SSA that may affect your eligibility to receive benefits. The SSA requires that all SSDI recipients report the following information while receiving SSDI benefits:

- Any work you perform, no matter the amount earned
- Any other disability benefits you receive
- If you participate in the Ticket to Work program
- If you move
- If your direct deposit account information changes
- If you need help managing your benefits
- If you receive a pension
- If there is a change in your marital or parental status

- If you are convicted of a crime, violate probation or parole or have an outstanding warrant for your arrest

Failure to provide this information, or providing false information, can result in the immediate termination of your benefits.

Can People on Social Security Disability Still Work?

The Social Security Administration understands that for many people in Illinois, their goal is to still work, despite their disability. For this reason, the SSA offers a set of special programs that are designed to help individuals remain in the workforce while still receiving disability benefits:

Ticket to Work Program

One of the programs available to disabled people is called the Ticket to Work program. This program can provide people with the following incentives to return to work:

- Rehabilitation, education or training for a new field
- Continued government medical insurance (Medicaid or Medicare)
- Cash benefits over a period of time

- Resumption of benefits if people are unable to continue working because of a worsened condition

When individuals use this program, it is important for them to keep the SSA informed of their work-related activities. Individuals in this program will not be subjected to any medical reviews if they follow the plan guidelines.

Income Limits

Individuals receiving Social Security Disability can work part-time without the income affecting their disability payments, as long as the total earnings are not more than $770 a month for an employed or self-employed person. Once a person exceeds that amount, they enter a trial work period (TWP) (described above). The TWP consists of nine months within a 60-month period, and there is no limit on income levels during this time.

Once someone has worked a total of nine months, they can enter into a second period, which is 36 months. In this extended work period, individual's benefits can be stopped or lowered if they earn more than $1,070 per month. That limit is raised to $1,800 for people who are blind.

Income Deductions

Work-related expenses that concern a person's disability may be able to be used as a deduction against a person's monthly income. Physical therapy to improve mobility, public transportation costs, prescription co-pays, special work equipment, wheelchairs, and therapy sessions may be eligible as a deduction. In these cases, the amount of money used to pay for these services would be subtracted from the person's monthly income, which means that a person could earn more than the income limit and still receive their benefits.

Reporting

As previously stated, keeping the SSA informed on work activity is important for people receiving disability benefits. In addition to informing the SSA about whether a person is or isn't working, people also need to ensure that the SSA is kept aware of the individual's income each month, as well as any other notifications involving their work. If you have questions about working while receiving disability, we recommend contacting an experienced attorney.

Tip: Be very careful about going back to work. If you miscalculate the amount of money you receive from work you could lose your SSD benefits permanently. Also, if SSA does a CDR of your case, they could conclude if you worked a little more you would not be disabled.

Disability Update Report

When it is time for your CDR, (continuing disability review) the SSA will mail you Form SSA-455, the Disability Update Report. This report usually covers the previous 24-month period, though it may be shorter; the exact period will be included on the report. This form requests information on the following:

- Your work history and monthly earnings
- Whether or not you have the ability to return to work
- Any improvement regarding your medical condition
- Whether or not you have been hospitalized or have seen a doctor for any type of treatment, and the reason for these visits

You must complete and submit the report to the address indicated within 30 days of receipt; failure to do so may result in termination of benefits. Once the form is returned, the SSA will let you know within 90 days whether benefits will continue or not, or if you must submit to a full medical review. Submitting any new medical documentation that supports your disability can help facilitate the review.

Continuing Disability Review Report

If the SSA determines it needs more information to review your case, it will send Form SSA-454, the Continuing Disability Review Report. This report is similar to the Disability Update Report, but it requires more in-depth information, including the names of all the physicians and hospitals you have visited since your last review. Sending these records with the report not only speeds up the process, but also ensures that the SSA gets all the records that support your disability. The SSA may also require you to have a consultative medical exam with an independent physician; in this case,the SSA will pay for the exam.

If Your Social Security Disability Benefits Are Terminated

If the SSA terminates your benefits following a CDR, you have the right to appeal the decision. As in the initial application process, there are four levels of review: reconsideration, hearing, appeals council review, and a federal lawsuit. The appeal must be filed within 60 days of receiving notice that your benefits were denied. If you wish to receive benefits during the appeals process, you must submit the appeal within ten days of receipt, and you must specifically request that benefits be paid during the appeals process. If your appeal is ultimately denied, you may be responsible for paying back any benefits paid during this time.

Medicare Coverage When You Receive SSDI Benefits

Disability recipients often want to know if they will also be able to receive health insurance, as many lose their health insurance by the time they are approved for disability by the Social Security Administration (SSA). This tends to be a concern, because people who are receiving Social Security Disability benefits often have pre-existing conditions. These conditions can prevent individuals from being able to obtain private health insurance, or these conditions can make the private health insurance available to them extremely expensive.

The Waiting Period

The SSA understands that its disability recipients need health insurance. However, the SSA does not make Medicare coverage immediately available to its disability recipients. Instead, the SSA requires a twenty-nine month waiting period for its disability recipients to begin receiving Medicare. This time frame is calculated as twenty-four months from the month you were first eligible to receive SSD benefits and not from the date that you became disabled.

Disability recipients who can continue their current health insurance should not drop their coverage at the time they begin receiving Social Security Disability payments. If it is possible for you to continue to keep your health insurance coverage during this two-year waiting period, you should try to do so to ensure that you maintain your health benefits. If you do not keep your current coverage, you may be without health insurance for up to two years.

You May Have Already Completed the Waiting Period

As explained above, the date of the two-year waiting period begins when you were first eligible to receive your monthly disability benefits. However, this does not mean that every person who is approved for SSD benefits will have to wait two years to receive Medicare coverage. The day you first become eligible to receive disability benefits may have been far enough in the past that you have already completed much or all of the two-year waiting period by the time you receive an award of benefits from the SSA. For example, it can take one to two years to get a disability decision when going through the appeals process.

Special Exceptions

There are also a couple of important exceptions to the two-year waiting period for Medicare benefits. If you suffer from one of these conditions, you can receive expedited Medicare coverage:

1.   End Stage Renal Disease with Kidney Failure

If you suffer from end-stage renal disease with kidney failure and require ongoing dialysis or need a kidney transplant, you can receive Medicare coverage starting the third month after your dialysis begins.

2.   Amyotrophic Lateral Sclerosis

If you suffer from amyotrophic lateral sclerosis, you are eligible to receive Medicare benefits as soon as you are eligible to receive disability benefits.

Are SSDI Benefits Taxable?

It depends on which type of SSD benefit an individual is getting. SSI benefits are not taxable, while Social Security Disability Insurance (SSDI) benefits are subject to tax.

Whether an SSDI recipient would pay taxes on his or her SSDI benefits depends on how much income the disability recipient makes in general. Most SSDI recipients do not make much income outside of what they receive in SSDI benefits, and, as a result, do not end up paying income tax on their SSDI benefits. However, about a third of the individuals receiving SSDI benefits do pay some taxes on their SSDI benefits because they have a higher total income.

Federal Tax on SSDI Benefits

Federal tax on SSDI benefits are related to a disability recipient's income and marital status. Below are charts with monthly income amounts to explain how much SSDI benefits may be taxed. Keep in mind that these charts explain the share of the person's benefits that would be subject to tax and that the share of those benefits would be taxed at the marginal income tax rate.

Single SSDI Recipient

If the SSDI recipient is single and has an income that is greater than $25,000 per year, a portion of his or her SSDI benefits will be subject to taxation.

Monthly Income Share of SSDI Benefits to be Taxed

$0-$2,083	None
$2,084-$2,833	Half of SSDI benefits will be taxed
$2,834 and up	85% of SSDI benefits will be taxed

Married SSDI Recipient

If the SSDI recipient is married, files taxes jointly with his or her spouse, and the couple has a combined income that is greater than $32,000 per year, a portion of the recipient's SSDI benefits will be subject to taxation.

Monthly Income Share of SSDI Benefits to be Taxed

$0-$2,666	None
$2,667-$3,666	Half of SSDI benefits will be taxed
$3,667 and up	85% of SSDI benefits will be taxed

State Tax on SSDI Benefits

The states that tax SSDI benefits include Connecticut, Colorado, Iowa, Kansas, Montana, Minnesota, Nebraska, North Dakota, Rhode Island, Utah, Vermont, and West Virginia.

Tax on Social Security Disability Back Pay

When large lump-sum back payments of SSDI benefits are made to recipients for the months the recipient was disabled but not yet approved for benefits, then these sums increase a recipient's annual income amount. This can cause disability recipients to pay a larger amount in taxes than they should in that year.

Disability recipients are allowed to apply the benefits owed from a previous year to prior tax returns, which lowers their income in the year the sum was received. If this applies to you, consider consulting an experienced attorney for more help with this issue.

Chapter 11

Complex Issues

The Importance of Worker's Compensation Spread Language

Perhaps you were injured on the job, and you've just received a workers' compensation settlement, payable in one big lump sum. You're thrilled—until a few weeks later, when you receive a letter from the SSA informing you that your monthly SSD benefits have been discontinued as a result of the settlement.

Perhaps you become disabled following an accident that is completely unrelated to the worker's compensation claim. The SSA eventually approves your application for SSDI benefits, only to immediately reduce your monthly benefits due to the workers' compensation award.

These situations could have been avoided if only the settlement agreement had included worker's compensation spread language.

> ## An Example of Spread Language is as Follows:
>
> After payment of attorney's fees and costs, petitioner will receive a net amount of $ ____. This payment is for a permanent impairment that will affect the petitioner for the rest of his or her life. The Social Security Administration's Actuarial Life Table indicates that petitioner, at age _____, has a life expectancy of _____ years, or _____ months. The amortized monthly net benefit is $ _____ per month. This represents future income replacement. This paragraph is intended for federal Social Security purposes only.

How Workers' Compensation Affects Social Security Disability Benefits

The SSA will reduce or eliminate monthly disability benefits if the recipient also receives a worker's compensation settlement. This offset occurs even if the medical condition that qualified the recipient for disability benefits is unrelated to the injury that resulted in the receipt of the workers' compensation benefits.

When a person receives both workers' compensation and SSDI benefits, the combined amount of these benefits—including SSDI benefits received by any member of the recipient's household—cannot exceed 80 percent of the recipient's average current earnings before he or she became disabled. To understand how this works, take the case of a 35-year-old man who received a $50,000 workers' compensation settlement after a construction site accident shattered his leg. Three months later, he is blinded as the result of a genetic eye disorder and is no longer able to work. Based on his disability, he is awarded $1,500 a month in SSDI benefits. His average monthly earnings at the time were $1,700.

The total amount of the SSDI and workers' compensation benefits exceed 80 percent of his average current earnings before becoming disabled. As a result, the SSA will offset the entire workers' compensation settlement against his $1,500 monthly disability benefit amount. The length of the offset is determined by dividing the workers' compensation settlement amount by the value of the monthly benefits. In this case, the recipient will be ineligible to receive disability payments for 34 months.

How the Inclusion of Worker's Compensation Spread Language Minimizes the Reduction of Benefits

Now, consider the above example again, but this time the workers' compensation settlement agreement contained spread language amortizing the payments over the recipient's life expectancy.

According to the SSA's life table, a 35-year-old man has a life expectancy of 43.10 years. Spreading the workers' compensation settlement over his life expectancy results in an award of approximately $97 per month.

The man's average monthly earnings prior to becoming disabled was $1,600; 80 percent of that amount is $1,280. The combined value of his $1,500 SSDI benefits per month and $97 workers' compensation payment exceeds 80 percent of his average current earnings by $317. ($1,600 x .80 = $1,280; $1,597 – $1,280 = $317)

Disability benefits will, therefore, be reduced by $317, leaving him with a $1,183 monthly benefit payment—a much better outcome than the $0 in disability payments he would have received absent the inclusion of spread language.

Because the SSA will reduce a recipient's monthly disability payment, even if the medical condition that justifies receipt of SSDI benefits is unrelated to the medical condition that resulted in receipt of the workers' compensation award, spread language should be included in all workers' compensation settlement agreements as a matter of course.

Can a Congressional Inquiry Help Your SSDI Claim?

When an applicant's SSDI claim has been denied initially and upon reconsideration, it can feel like there is little hope for obtaining SSDI benefits. Though the appeals process can provide these applicants with additional avenues to pursue, often applicants have difficulty waiting for a disability hearing to be scheduled due to a financial or medical hardship. This is because, after a request for a hearing has been made, it can take months to get the hearing date scheduled.

In these cases, asking for a congressional inquiry can provide a helpful boost to a denied applicant's case. A congressional inquiry is a status check on your disability application that your local senator or representative makes on your behalf.

How to Initiate a Congressional Inquiry

If an applicant wishes to initiate a congressional inquiry, he or she first needs to contact his or her local senator or representative's office to request that the congressperson look into where the applicant's claim stands in the disability process. When making the request, the applicant should give the congressperson enough information to understand the applicant's claim and the general circumstances surrounding the applicant's concerns.

The issues to tell your congressperson about, include:

1. How long you have been involved in the SSDI application process

2. How long you have already waited for an appeal hearing to be scheduled

3. The number of dependents or family members you are currently supporting

4. Any stress the disability application has caused you in particular, such as medical, emotional, or financial distress

5. Any other reasons that will help explain to your congressperson why you need a congressional inquiry.

What Happens After You Request a Congressional Inquiry

If your congressperson accepts your request and takes action on your behalf, he or she will contact the SSA to ask for an update on the status of your SSDI claim. The congressperson's office may call or send a written notice to the SSA to ask for the update. The SSA also has specific rules it must follow regarding how to respond to a congressional inquiry. This action may push the SSA to resolve your claim sooner, but such positive results are not guaranteed.

It is very important to remember that, while a congressional inquiry may speed up the SSDI application process, it will not impact the SSA's decision regarding whether or not you are eligible for benefits. A congressional inquiry cannot influence the outcome of an application, because that is still entirely dependent on the applicant's medical records and his or her functional limitations.

While congressional inquiries do not cause SSDI applications to be approved, they do help get applications moving faster along the approval process. Asking for a congressional inquiry cannot negatively impact your case, and congressional inquiries can be worth pursuing.

What Money Can Be Taken from SSDI Payments and Social Security Payments?

SSDI benefits are meant to help disabled workers when they need it most. For this reason, these benefits come with some built-in protections so that creditors cannot take these benefits from workers who need them.

In most circumstances, creditors cannot garnish wages from a disabled worker's Social Security Disability Insurance (SSDI) payments and Social Security payments. However, there are still a few exceptions that disability claimants should be aware of when applying for benefits.

Child Support

Some but not all disability benefits can be taken to pay a disability recipient's child support. SSDI benefits can be taken for this purpose, but not Supplemental Security Income (SSI) benefits. This is because SSDI is a disability benefit that is earned by a worker over time, while SSI benefits are need-based and given to low-income individuals. As a result, SSDI benefits are considered as income when calculating child support, while SSI benefits are not calculated in the same way.

Alimony

Most state courts do not consider SSDI benefits to be marital property during divorce proceedings when marital assets are being divided. However, as with child support, SSDI benefits are considered income when determining alimony awards, while SSI benefits are not.

Bankruptcy

Because disability recipients need their SSDI payments to live on, these benefits are protected in Chapter 7 bankruptcy, but there are some exceptions. Whether a disability recipient can keep all of his or her SSDI payments or not depends on where the disability recipient lives, whether or not the disability recipient gets payments from any other source, and whether or not the disability recipient is trying to protect past or future disability payments.

When is a Decision Final?

The SSA's rules state that a SSD determination cannot be reopened after 12 months without good cause. Even with good cause, applicants only have four years from the decision date to request that a determination be revisited. A decision is final after this deadline. However, applicants who failed to request review within the relevant deadlines due to mental incapacity or other good cause may be eligible for extensions.

Incapacity or Good Cause

The SSA considers each situation to determine whether or not there is good cause for reopening a claim. The SSA may consider the reasons the applicant failed to reopen the claim before, the potential role the SSA's actions played, and the applicant's ability to understand the relevant rules.

An applicant may qualify for a deadline extension if the applicant suffers from a mental limitation that prevented him or her from understanding the review process. The SSA may consider the following factors when evaluating mental incapacity:

- The applicant's level of education
- The applicant's ability to communicate in English
- The applicant's literacy or ability to speak

- The disabling conditions that limit the applicant's ability to perform tasks independently

These factors are only relevant if the applicant lacked a legal representative, such as a parent or attorney, who was responsible for pursuing the claim. The SSA typically will not grant an extension because of a representative's mistakes or oversights. However, if an applicant lacks a representative and has significant mental incapacity, the claim decision may be reopened, regardless of how much time has passed.

Reconsidering Claim Decisions

When revisiting a past decision, a Social Security adjudicator must obtain as much evidence as possible. The adjudicator must assist the applicant in acquiring the relevant evidence if the applicant still lacks a legal representative. If reasonable doubt remains after the evidence is gathered, the adjudicator must decide the issue in the applicant's favor.

If the adjudicator finds the applicant does not have good cause for a deadline extension, the adjudicator will dismiss the request for review. If the applicant chooses to file a new claim, the original request for reconsideration can serve as a written notice of intent to file for benefits. This establishes a protective filing date, even if the application is not filed until later. A protective filing date ensures that applicants do not lose eligibility for SSDI benefits while they wait to file a claim. It may also help applicants qualify for greater retroactive benefits if the new claim is ultimately approved.

Losing Social Security Disability Benefits

People in Illinois may believe that once they are approved to receive benefits for their disability from Social Security, they are in the clear. However, it is important to understand that benefits can be withdrawn.

Health Condition Improves

After the approval of Social Security Disability benefits is given, the Social Security Administration will still conduct continuing reviews of people's conditions. The frequency of these reviews depends on how permanent the condition is or the recipient's age. For example, someone with a treatable disability, like fibromyalgia, may experience a review every couple of years while someone who is paralyzed with permanent nerve damage could receive a review every six years.

If a review shows that the person's condition has improved and that the symptoms of the condition no longer meet the qualifying criteria for SSDI benefits, then the SSA will terminate those benefits. People will receive a notice for an upcoming review by mail, and it is a good idea to make sure that the SSA receives updated medical information to show that the benefits are still necessary.

Returning to Work

People who are on disability and return to work run the risk of losing their benefits. The SSA has clear guidelines about how much a person can earn each month and still receive benefits. However, people can use what is called a trial work period which extends over a nine-month period during a 60-month period. If people on disability work longer than a summary of nine months, they could lose their disability.

The SSA establishes an income limit of $1,070 each month for disabled people. However, each person's situation can be different, and people may be able to earn more than this amount without it hurting their benefits. When examining income amounts, the SSA does include free food and housing.

Retirement

People on disability will automatically lose their disability benefits when they reach retirement age. However, the loss of disability is transferred over to regular Social Security. This may or may not affect the amount that someone receives. However, people at, and over the retirement age, are no longer eligible for the disability program.

Questioning Benefits Cancellation

When the SSA cancels someone's disability benefits, that person has the right and the option to file an appeal. The person must submit the appeal request within 60 days of the cancellation letter having been received. The person can ask for benefits to be paid out during the appeal process, but if the appeal is denied, they may have to pay back some or all of the benefits received. Due to the complexity of the SSA appeal process, individuals would benefit from an experienced Illinois disability attorney's advice.

Medical Treatment Log

Use the log on the following pages to track your medical treatment. The closer you track it, the easier it is for your attorney to obtain the necessary medical records for your case. Try to be as specific as possible, as this will help your attorney gather the records for your case.

Date of Appointment	Doctor/ Hospital Name	Reason for Visit

Date of Appointment	Doctor/ Hospital Name	Reason for Visit

Date of Appointment	Doctor/ Hospital Name	Reason for Visit

Date of Appointment	Doctor/ Hospital Name	Reason for Visit

Date of Appointment	Doctor/ Hospital Name	Reason for Visit

Glossary

Application for Disability Insurance Benefits (Form SSA-16- BK): This is the form that starts a claimant's Social Security Disability case.

Adult Disability Report- Form SSA-3368- BK: This report was created to get detailed information regarding a claimant's work history, earnings history, and medical condition.

Authorization to Disclose Information (Form SSA 827): Allows the SSA to request and receive information about a claimant's medical history in addition to other confidential information.

Case Evaluation: A case evaluation performed by an attorney's office helps an attorney to determine whether the claimant is disabled based on the Social Security rules and if the claimant has a chance to qualify for SSD benefits.

Compassionate Allowance: Allows the SSA to target those claimants who are the most disabled and allows for disability benefits to be granted to those persons soon after they apply for SSD benefits.

Continuing Disability Review ("CDR"): A review conducted by the SSA to determine if an applicant is still eligible to receive Social Security Disability Benefits. You will receive form Form SSA-455, the Disability Update Report, from the SSA to complete and return within 30 days of receipt.

Impairment Listings: Blue book impairment listings contain guidelines for evaluating specific medical conditions.

Medical Source Statement: A document that helps prove your claim that your disability negatively impacts your ability to work.

Medical Vocational Grids: These establish rules for determining a claimant's ability to work.

Onset Date: The date a claimant became disabled.

Residual Functional Capacity: This is an assessment of what kind of work the claimant is able to do and what the claimant is too limited to do due to their disability.

Social Security Disability Back Pay: The monthly benefit owed to a claimant from the onset of his disability until he is awarded benefits.

Social Security Disability Work Credits: The SSA converts your job earnings into work credits to decide whether a claimant has worked long enough to qualify for SSD benefits.

Social Security Function Report- Form SSA3373: A questionnaire required by the SSA for applicants to complete that helps the SSA determine the severity of impact that your disability has on your ability to conduct daily work/life functions.

Technical Denial: A claimant will receive a technical denial when she does not meet the SSA's basic, non-medical criteria for SSD benefits.

Third Party Function Report- Form SSA-3380-BK: A form used by the SSA to help determine how the claimant's disability affects their ability to work and perform daily functions, completed by a third party.

Worker's Compensation Spread Language: Used to allow the workers' compensation payment to be amortized over his life expectancy.

Work History Report- Form SSA-3369- BK: This form requests details about a claimant's job duties and the impact your disability has on your ability to perform said duties. It also requests information on wages, education and any job training.

About the Authors

Shawn M. Good and Neil H. Good are a father-and-son attorney team. Shawn and Neil joined together to form The Good Law Group to combine their shared passion for helping people as lawyers. The Good Law serves Social Security Disability claimants throughout the Chicago, Illinois metro area and surrounding areas with passion, skill, and zeal.

For over 25 years, our founding attorney, Neil H. Good, has made sure that our firm provides effective and efficient Social Security Disability assistance to disabled and ill clients throughout the Chicago, Illinois, area as well as nationally on a case by case basis.

Neil H. Good speaks on topics related to Social Security Disability benefits and Supplemental Security Income to hospital support groups, health groups, township services organizations, social services organizations, community groups and others.

Having grown up following in his father's footsteps, Shawn Good knew from a young age that he wanted to be an attorney. Shawn is a highly organized, hardworking and zealous advocate for those in need. He is admitted to the Illinois state bar, the Northern

District of Illinois, and the Seventh Circuit Court of Appeals.

If you would like to schedule a free presentation and question-and-answer session about SSD and SSI, please contact us a: 847-250-9183 or info@thegoodlawgroup.com

About the Artist

As a child, Troy Kowalski always knew he had a different set of skills. He suffered from a hearing deficit which made him concentrate more on visuals for learning and communication. Troy developed an interest in art after watching his Mom, Laura Kowalski, who was an artist working in pottery and watercolors. In 1998, his passion for art grew when his mother passed away from a long battle with Breast Cancer.

Growing up, Troy experimented with various mediums such as pastels, graphite, spray paint, acrylic, color pencils, and watercolors. He never limited his creativity to just paper. He started airbrushing clothing and at the age of 18, Troy had his first art show in Chicago, IL.

In 2013, Troy graduated from Illinois State University with a Bachelor's of Science in Graphic Design. During his undergrad, he did illustrations for children's story books, wall murals around campus, and t-shirts for campus events.

Throughout Troy's full-time experience with COUNTRY Financial, RR Donnelley, Winix America Inc., and a few design studios, Troy continues to take on design projects, commissioned illustrations, and custom paintings. His goal is to touch others with power, motivation, and inspiration through his art and graphics for many years to come.

Troy can be reached at: troykowalski8@gmail.com

To view Troy's other work, go to:
www.troykowalski.com